Classroom Practice in Reading

105197

Richard A. Earle, Editor
McGill University

ira International Reading Association
Newark, Delaware 19711

INTERNATIONAL READING ASSOCIATION

OFFICERS
1977-1978

Copyright 1977 by the
International Reading Association, Inc.
Library of Congress Cataloging in Publication Data
Earle, Richard A.
    Classroom practice in reading.
    Bibliography: p.
    1. Reading. 2. Oral reading. I. Title.
LB1050.E195   428.4'07   77-24101
ISBN 0-87207-482-X

LB
1050
.E 195

CONTENTS

6-9-78 alumni 4.00

Foreword

Through the organization he has given to **Classroom Practice in Reading,** Richard Earle emphasizes the need for the teacher to take a systematic approach to meeting the instructional needs of different individuals and different groups. There is considerable evidence that the practice of defining what is to be learned, and then evaluating and attending to the gaps in each learner's preparation, can result in a substantial increase in the number of students who make the desired gains. If readers of this volume will apply to teaching the organizing principles the editor develops, this publication will make a significant contribution to the effectiveness of school learning.

Through the selection of articles in this booklet, Dr. Earle broadens our understanding of each of the steps in the diagnostic/prescriptive model of teaching. For example, we are immediately informed that teaching can have affective as well as cognitive purposes. Evaluation includes far more than tests. The materials we choose or prepare involve considerations ranging from vocabulary selection to affective impact. The concept of method implies much more than a certain underlying emphasis; the concept can encourage us to consider a wide range of both specific activities and organizing concepts to accomplish varied purposes at different times with different students. If readers will apply to teaching the broad range of ideas the editor introduces, this volume will make a significant contribution to the liveliness of school learning.

Walter H. MacGinitie, President
International Reading Association
1976-1977

INSTRUCTIONAL READING

Perspective One

This volume focuses on classroom practice specific to the instructional program in reading, that is, the direct teaching of reading skills or processes. It is organized according to a diagnostic/prescriptive model of classroom instruction comprised of five major steps in a sound instructional sequence.

The sequence begins with the identification of **Instructional Purpose**, at which point each teacher makes a definite (if not definitive) statement describing the reading process, based on all available information.

This sense of instructional purpose will dictate in large part the next step in the sequence, the **Evaluation** or diagnosis of student reading strengths and needs.

The results of this formative evaluation will help the teacher select, purchase, or make instructional **Materials** which serve as vehicles for teaching.

In addition to materials, the teacher needs instructional **Methods** which serve the instructional needs of individuals and groups within the class.

Diagnostic information and the multiple prescriptions that follow must then be implemented through effective classroom **Management,** which includes accurate records and continuous evaluation of student growth.

Each of the five sections in this volume is devoted to one of the instructional components mentioned above. The introduction to each section defines the step in more detail and shows how it is related to the rest of the sequence. Articles follow which present a sampling of ideas on that topic. Additional sources for further information on the topic complete each of the sections.

Each paper included in this volume can help the classroom teacher develop further expertise with at least one of the five diagnostic/prescriptive components described. None of the papers can be considered complete in its treatment of any single component, however. Nor can its companion articles, or indeed any single volume such as this, make a reasonable claim for such comprehensiveness. Therefore, the reader—to gain maximum value from this collection—should first examine closely the diagnostic/prescriptive model itself. A grasp of the model will provide the reader with a useful framework for organizing present knowledge and for acquiring, judging, and assimilating ideas presented by the various authors represented herein.

RAE

Instructional Purpose

Success in teaching depends first of all on a clearly defined instructional purpose. For reading teachers this means coming to terms with the complex question, "What is fluent reading?" The process of reading may never be defined completely. Nonetheless, each of us at every level of instruction must examine all available evidence and arrive at a tentative decision. That decision—or the lack of it—will be reflected in every aspect of classroom practice. With some reasonable teacher definition of mature reading behavior, instruction can proceed toward that goal; without it, instruction will be without focus, without purpose, without meaning.

What conclusions have you reached about reading? Is it merely the recognition and pronunciation of written symbols? Does it include the discernment of meaning at one or more levels? What roles do interest and attitude play in fluent reading behavior? Does reading mean the mastery of a set of identifiable universal skills? Or is reading behavior a complex mix of perceptual, cognitive, and linguistic experience which operates only in combination with personal purpose and individual style?

For your consideration, this section presents two points of view— **not to replace** but to enhance and enlarge your present definition of reading.

Planning the Affective Component

DARRYL J. STRICKLER
Indiana University

What have they gained if children leave school knowing how to read, but don't know why to read, what to read, when to read—or worse—don't care to read at all? **(1)**

Children who complete their formal education knowing how to read, but not "why to read, when to read, and what to read" have probably been exposed to a less than complete reading instructional program. In addition to providing for children's reading skill needs, a balanced reading program must include a well-planned "affective component" which provides for the development of interests, attitudes, and personal values in relation to reading for information and enjoyment.

Goals and Objectives

The planning of any instructional program component should begin with a clear statement of the overall purpose or major goal of the program. It is suggested that the major goal of the reading instructional program, whether a schoolwide or an individual teacher's program, should be to help each child develop purposeful and personally con-structive reading habits—in other words, the kind of reading habits, either informational or recreational, which serve a purpose the reader has established for himself and which contribute to his personal growth and understanding. Teaching children how to read will only partially help them to attain this major goal. If children are to develop reading habits that will serve them throughout their lives, they must experience the excitement, the personal fulfillment, and the practical value of learning which can be attained through reading.

The following objectives for the affective component of the reading program are directly related to the major goal of helping children develop purposeful and personally constructive reading habits.

    1.0 **Awareness.** The student will be aware of the various purposes which reading can serve. He/she will

        1.1 be aware of the information gathering potential of reading

        1.2 be aware of the enjoyment which can be derived

through the reading of literature
- 1.3 be aware of the opportunities for personal growth which reading provides
- 2.0 **Interest.** The student will demonstrate an active interest in reading as an information gathering process and as a source of enjoyment and self-fulfillment. He/she will
  - 2.1 consider using books and other printed media as sources of information
  - 2.2 actively attend to, and derive enjoyment from, literature being read to or by him/her
  - 2.3 actively seek out and examine books and other printed matter to explore their potential for fulfillment of personal needs
- 3.0 **Attitude.** The student will demonstrate a positive attitude toward reading and reading instruction. He/she will
  - 3.1 frequently engage in recreational reading when faced with a number of equally attractive alternatives for use of leisure time
  - 3.2 frequently use reading as a means of gathering information, deriving knowledge, and seeking understanding
  - 3.3 actively participate in learning activities designed to increase reading skills
- 4.0 **Value.** The student will incorporate reading into his/her personal value system. He/she will
  - 4.1 develop his/her own purposes for reading in relation to his/her personal value system
  - 4.2 identify and read specific literature which is related to his/her personal value system
  - 4.3 effectively use various resources to locate literature and other printed media related to his/her enjoyment and information needs

In order to reflect the developmental nature of reading habits, the objectives listed above have been arranged in a four-stage hierarchy or taxonomy. The arrangement of the subobjectives in a taxonomy suggests that, before a child can achieve the major goal of developing purposeful and personally constructive reading habits, he goes through various stages of affective development in relation to reading and literature. For example, the child must first be aware of the informational and recreational purposes which reading can serve (1.0 **Awareness**). As his awareness of the purposes of reading develops, his interest and attitude toward reading begin to form (2.0 **Interest** and 3.0 **Attitude**). It is at the interest and attitude levels in the child's affective development in reading that the elementary school reading program can exert the greatest influence. (Obviously, the influence of the reading program can be in a positive or negative direction.) If the influence is in a positive direction, it is more likely that the child will incorporate reading and literature into his personal system of values (4.0 **Value**), and ultimately achieve the major goal of developing purposeful and personally constructive reading habits.

Although the above description of the taxonomy of subobjectives serves as a simplistic example of a child's affective development in reading, in reality the development of reading habits is a long and complicated process involving many interrelated variables.

Assessing Affective Development

A crucial step in helping children to attain the objectives listed is to gather, on an ongoing basis, adequate informtion relevant to each child's probable level of affective development in relation to reading. Such information serves as the basis for selecting appropriate strategies, resources, and activities for each child.

The concept of "diagnostic teaching" has particular relevance in relation to discovering children's levels of affective development, since the most useful information about interests and attitudes must be gathered daily by the teacher. Every school day allows countless opportunities for observant teachers to determine children's interests and attitudes. Conversations between children, products of their creative activities, class projects, trips to the library, group sharing activities, and a variety of other situations in which children are involved in self-initiated activities, provide rich sources of information about their interests and attitudes toward reading. The teacher who is aware of the opportunities which all of these situations provide will not only make a concerted effort to observe and interact with children in a variety of learning situations, but also will record those observations on a daily or weekly basis.

Time spent with one child examining and discussing various books in the school or classroom library can not only provide the teacher with greater insight into the child's interests and attitudes toward reading, but also can communicate to the child the teacher's genuine concern and interest in him as a person.

Without question, the best way to determine a child's interests and attitudes is by getting to know him well. And while there is no real substitute for first-hand knowledge about the child (gathered through informal observation and interaction), there are various techniques and specific instruments which a teacher can use to assess children's interests and attitudes. Interest inventories, attitude questionnaires, structured and informal interviews, observation checklists, circulation records from school and classroom libraries, records of books the child has read, and autobiographies written by the child, can all provide sources of valuable information about the child.

Regardless of how it is gathered, information about the child's interests and attitudes must be used to plan the affective component of the reading program. Once the teacher has determined the child's probable level of affective development in relation to reading, appropriate strategies, techniques, activities and resources can be selected and utilized to further this development.

Selecting Strategies and Resources

When children begin school they bring with them a wide variety of reading-related concepts, interests, attitudes, and values which might be viewed as the raw material from which reading habits develop. And although we as teachers may have little control over the concepts, interests, attitudes, and values which children have when they begin school, we can play a major role in influencing the kind of reading habits children will take with them when they leave school.

Many strategies and resources can be used successfully to develop reading interests, attitudes, and values. Following is a list of the basic assumptions upon which the use of these strategies and resources are based:

1. One of the primary objectives for the elementary school reading program is to aid the individual child in his development of purposeful and personally constructive reading habits.

2. An individual's reading habits can be influenced by providing him with appropriate reading and literature related activities and experiences within the elementary school setting.

3. A primary means of affecting interest in reading (and, consequently, constructive reading habits) is by determining an individual's interests so that reading instruction materials and reading and literature related experiences can be provided which are based on those interests.

4. The interests, attitudes, and personal values an individual has in relation to reading exert a significant influence upon his reading habits.

5. The degree to which an individual discovers personal relevance and value in what he reads will, to a large extent, influence his attitude toward reading and, in turn, his reading habits.

After considering and evaluating the above assumptions in relation to his own personal and professional value system, the basic question that remains for the teacher is, "How do you turn kids on to reading?" Just as there is no single approach which has been found to be consistently more effective than another approach in teaching children how to read, there also is no single most effective approach for developing children's interests, attitudes, and values in relation to reading. For this reason, many approaches and strategies for affective development should be tried and should become part of the teacher's repertoire.

Guidelines for Classroom Practice

The following guidelines for developing children's reading interests, attitudes, and values are suggested for the teacher. Some of these guidelines refer to aspects of the elementary school reading/language arts program, some refer to the classroom climate for reading, and others, imply specific teacher behaviors which encourage children to read independently.

1. **Use children's interests in planning instruction.** Get to know each of your students well. Determine each child's interests and provide reading and literature related activities and materials which are based on those interests.
2. **Assure the child's success in the mastery of reading skills and strategies.** Develop needed skills sequentially, teaching only those skills which have not been mastered previously. Make learning how to read enjoyable. Show the child that his listening and speaking skills help him in his reading and writing skills.
2. **Help the child discover his own purposes for reading.** Show him that reading is not just a subject in the school curriculum but a valuable tool for expanding and clarifying his own experiences. Help him learn why, when, and what to read, as well as how to read.
4. **Read often to children.** Set aside time in the schedule to read to children on a regular basis. Expose them to creative and colorful use of language in poetry and narrative. Introduce

them to the sounds and rhythms of language. Select what you read to children with the same care you use in selecting your own reading material.

5. **Carefully select books for your literature program.** Become familiar with the best in children's literature. Use your knowledge of children's books to select books for your classroom library and to recommend specific books to your students. Use children's literature to supplement learning of, and interest in, content areas of the curriculum (for example, social studies and science).

6. **Be an enthusiastic model of reading habits.** Share with children your enthusiasm for reading and books. Be seen reading for your own enjoyment.

7. **Fill the bookshelves in your classroom.** Stock your classroom with a great quantity and quality of books and other printed matter, especially paperback books. Beg, buy, borrow, or make books; but by all means have them available for the children.

8. **Provide time for independent reading.** Allow time within your schedule for sustained silent reading of student selected reading materials.

9. **Encourage children to read and share what they have read.** Set up "sharing" and "celebrating" activities through which children can stimulate the interests of their classmates.

10. **Develop a literature program.** Design a literature program which will help children realize the potential literature holds for widening their world.

The guidelines listed above can encompass many specific strategies and techniques for developing children's reading interests, attitudes, and values.

Conclusion

This brief guide for planning the affective component of the reading program has suggested specific objectives, assessment techniques, and general guidelines for the selection and utilization of strategies and resources. If creatively used, the suggestions can serve as the basis for planning an effective reading instructional program component which provides for children's affective development in, and through, reading.

References

1. Strickler, Darryl J., and William Eller. "Reading: Attitudes and Interests," Chapter 13 in Pose Lamb and Richard Arnold (Eds.), **Reading: Foundations and Instructional Strategies.** Belmont, California: Wadsworth Publishing, 1976, 449-490.
2. Strickler, Darryl J. "The Affective Dimension of Reading," Section 5 in **Reading Effectiveness Program/Elementary School Guide.** Indianapolis: Indiana Department of Public Instruction, 1975.

Cognitive Style and the Reading Process

SYLVIA ROSENFIELD
Fordham University

Research on reading as a cognitive task has focused on reading as an active process involving complex strategies of information selection and processing (22). A set of related variables, which may prove useful in clarifying how these strategies operate, is available in the literature on cognitive style, the study of the unique tactics an individual develops to cope with information. The construct of cognitive style has developed in a number of directions (6, 20, 23). Two of these, the dimensions of global-analytic style and reflection-impulsivity, will serve to illustrate how cognitive style can increase understanding of reading as cognitive process.

Global-Analytic Cognitive Style

Kagan, Moss, and Sigel (13) describe an analytic child as one who tends to "analyze and differentiate the stimulus environment," in contrast to a global child who will categorize on the basis of "the stimulus as a whole" (p. 74). To discover the child's style, the Conceptual Style Test (CST) was developed. The CST requires the child to decide which two of three black and white pictures go together; the child can choose to group on the basis of a similar detail or a more global similarity. Kagan, et al. (13) suggested that an analytic attitude may facilitate acquiring early reading skills: "To notice the differences between 'cat' and 'bat' and 'dog' and 'bag' requires differentiation and analysis of the stimulus" (p. 111). Research by the author (19) supported the positive relationship between analytic-global style and word discrimination for male kindergarten children.

Reflection-Impulsivity

A correlate of an analytic-global style is response time. Analytic children were found to exhibit longer response times on the CST and, in his research, Kagan focused increasingly on the stable individual differences in response times in situations where several alternatives are available and there is some uncertainty as to which one is correct. The experimental task most often used to measure this variable is a test

(15) called Matching Familiar Figures (MFF). The format of the task involves presenting a standard and four, six, or eight figures differing in one or more details, except for one figure which is exactly the same as the standard. The subject is required to find the latter. Measures are obtained of time to first response and number of errors. Children above the median on response time and below the median on errors are termed **reflective**; children below the median on response time and above the median on errors are termed **impulsive** (see Figure 1). These two categories account for about two-thirds of most samples; children who are fast-accurate and those who are slow-inaccurate must be considered as other style types.

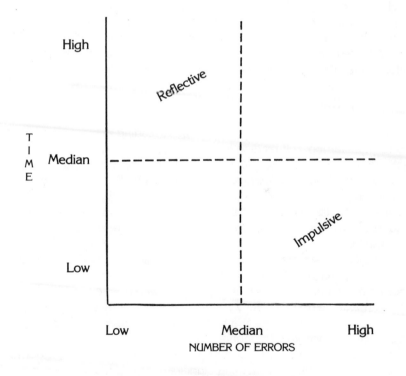

Figure 1.   Time-error score combinations suggesting reflective-impulsive children

Kagan (12) found that reflective children were able to learn letters and words more easily than children with an impulsive disposition. In a later publication, Kagan (11) notes that the child with a reading disability is more apt to be impulsive than reflective. Recently, Elkin and Briggs (5) uncovered a relationship between MFF error scores and early readers.

Cognitive Style and the Reading Process

How can the correlational relationships between reading and cognitive style be explained? If one concentrates on the perceptual componets of the reading process at the early stages of reading acquisition, there are several levels on which cognitive style might affect reading. First, examine a typical matching words or letters type of item common to most readiness tests. There is a clear similarity between such a task and the MFF format; for example, a child is presented a standard with a number of alternatives and is asked to find the alternative that matches the standard. One might expect children with impulsive tempos to respond to such a task quickly and with a high error rate. Rather than hypothesize a visual perceptual deficit of possible neurological origin, it may be more important to determine the response style of the child.

However, more than a surface similarity can be postulated between type of task used to measure both reading achievement and conceptual tempo 1) if reading is redefined, for children who are in the acquisition stage, as a task with high response uncertainty; and 2) if one agrees with Gibson (7: 352) that a child needs to discover "distinctive and invariant" features, extracting them from the "multiplicity of information in the flowing array of stimulation." How do an impulsive child and a reflective child differ in the way they search for relevant perceptual information?

Using a sample of second grade children, McKinney (16) examined perceptual tasks in which the correct response could be located by asking questions that could be answered yes or no. Reflective children extracted significantly more information with their questions than did impulsive children, and they were more likely to test the relevance of conceptual categories than specific instances. On the other hand, impulsive children tended to process information in a random, trial and error fashion. Something significant seems to happen during the additional time reflective children take before responding.

Ault, Crawford, and Jeffrey (1) suggest that by third grade, while visual scanning strategies are not significantly different in type between impulsive and reflective children, reflective and fast-accurate children are more systematic and make a greater proportion of comparisons than impulsive and slow-inaccurate children. The scanning or search strategies of reflective children involve greater concentration on finding similar parts of the variants, while the impulsive children are less systematic, more global. Impulsive children "do not scan the field for distinctive features as systemtically as do reflectives" (17:19).

Unquestionably, the reflective child uses more mature problem solving strategies. There is also a tendency for reflectivity to increase with age (10). Do the style differences simply reflect a difference in underlying intellectual capacity? In his review of the literature on impulsivity-reflection, Messer (17), scanned studies for correlations between MFF response time, errors, and IQ. He found a median correlation of .165, between MFF response time and IQ for both sexes, with a somewhat higher correlation between MFF errors and IQ (−.295 for boys and −.335 for girls). Apparently, conceptual tempo does not have a strong relationship to IQ in the normal range, although there is a higher correlation for errors than for response time and the relationship is somewhat stronger for girls than for boys.

Implications for Instruction

Berliner and Cahen (2:58) emphasize the need to determine those instructional factors that are especially helpful for particular subgroups of learners: "Given this set of learner characteristics, which is the best way to tailor instruction **for this particular type of learner**" [emphasis in original]. If there are critical aspects of style related to the reading process, this should lead to the development of better teaching and/or remedial procedures to either alter the cognitive structures involved or train an individual to read by a different method. A number of early studies (3, 14) chose to modify the cognitive style of the child by increasing response times for impulsive children on a variety of tasks. The results of these studies suggest that, while response time is modifiable, more specific intervention is needed to help the child use the increase in response latency to reduce error scores.

Several programs, still in experimental stages, have been developed which attempt to change perceptual information processing strategies in impulsive children. Robertson and Keeley (18) developed a procedure with first and second grade children to improve problem solving. Developed for a classroom setting, the authors constructed a reinforcement (social and token) program in which points were earned for attention, adherence to the procedure, and correct task completion.

The unique aspect of the program was a set of self-instructions, which the model first demonstrated and then instructed the child to follow. The children were taught how to mediate a more reflective approach to a cognitive task. The procedure included a set of five cards which helped the child recall the instructions. The cards read: 1) stop, listen, look, think; 2) what do I do? 3) slow, think, talk; 4) stop. O.K.? 5) good. The initial study with five subjects showed that the training reduced impulsive errors on a variety of measures and affected achievement for some of the children.

Another experimental curriculum designed by Egeland, Wozniak, and Thibodeau (4) consists of teaching children to focus on part-whole relationships, to plan the way they look at a visual array, and to combine the skills to solve match-to-sample problems similar to MFF tasks. The child is taught to focus on different types of distinctive features which are useful in determining whether a variant is the same or different from the standard figure.

While general problem solving strategies can be taught, there is also the alternative of developing techniques for teaching reading which consider a given child's cognitive style. Williams (22: 360) suggests that we do have some knowledge of what a good reading program should be:

> It is structured and organized; it minimizes possibilities of failure; it starts with simple, high contrast, highly cued items and progresses toward complex items which have stringent response requirements.

This approach seems particularly appropriate for children who respond with high error rates to situations of response uncertainty.

The importance of minimizing incorrect responses has been stressed in the behavioral literature. The technique of errorless learning (21), for example, teaches individuals to discriminate while keeping errors to a minimum. A child is presented with only one stimulus and his responses to it are reinforced. An alternate stimulus, which is not reinforced, is gradually introduced. Initially, the alternate is presented briefly and its characteristics are kept very different from the correct response. As training progresses, the alternate begins to resemble the correct response more, yet the child continues to respond only to the correct one. The possibilities for teaching such difficult discriminations as b and d through this method have only begun to be explored. Errorless learning offers a potential teaching technique for impulsive children in particular.

Another tack for training the early perceptual skills necessary for reading involves the use of extended discrimination practice, and it is based on the position that extended practice is useful (9). While Gibson and others (**8**:905) acknowledge that helping a child to attend to the distinctive features of letters can hardly hurt, they suggest that

> ...the child learns which varying dimensions of letters are significant and which are not by simply looking repeatedly at many samples containing both varying and invariant features.

In a study exploring whether this method could be applied to children with different cognitive styles, a discrimination practice program using a game approach was devised. Boys with global cognitive style improved their discrimination skills more than the other groups (**19**). It is possible that impulsive and global children need more practice with perceptual discriminations than our current reading programs offer in order to find the distinctive features they need.

Conclusions

The relationship between cognitive style and reading has been examined in terms of an underlying information processing strategy in perceptual learning. Apparently, children with an impulsive cognitive style are not as likely to succeed in perceptual discrimination tasks as those with a reflective style. In all instances, however, it may not be more efficient to be reflective. We need research to determine if impulsive children can read faster than reflective children, once response uncertainty has been reduced. It may be important , as well, to examine the relationship between cognitive style and such variables as fluency, expressiveness, and creativity (**24**).

In the early stages of learning to read, certain perceptual strategies are useful to the child as he works to discover the distinctive features to which he must attend. This paper has reviewed several possible ways to facilitate the cognitive processing of the impulsive or global child which can be adapted to the classroom. Currently, a number of skills are evaluated in early screening tests to find children with potential learning problems. Perhaps we need to add a measure of cognitive style to such batteries and be prepared to adjust our teaching methodology accordingly.

References

1. Ault, Ruth, David Crawford, and W.E. Jeffrey. "Visual Scanning Strategies of Reflective, Impulsive Fast-Accurate, and Slow-Inaccurate Children on the Matching Familiar Figures Test," **Child Development,** 43 (December 1972), 1412-1417.
2. Berliner, David, and Leonard Cahen. "Trait-Treatment Interaction and Learning," in F. Kerlinger (Ed.), **Review of Research in Education,** Volume 1. Itasca, Illinois: F. E. Peacock, 1973, 58-94.

3. Briggs, Chari, and Richard Weinberg. "Effects of Reinforcement in Training Children's Conceptual Tempos," **Journal of Educational Psychology,** 65 (December 1973), 383-394.
4. Egeland, Byron, Robert Wozniak, and Anne Thibodeau. "Visual Information Processing Training Program: Experimental Version," paper presented at Division 16 Preconvention Institute, American Psychological Association, August 1974.
5. Elkind, David, and Chari Briggs. "Cognitive Development in Early Readers," **Developmental Psychology,** 9 (September 1973), 279-280.
6. Gardner, Riley, et al. "Cognitive Control: A Study of Individual Consistencies in Cognitive Behavior," **Psychological Issues,** 1 (1959), 1-185.
7. Gibson, Eleanor. "Perceptual Learning and the Theory of Word Perception," **Cognitive Psychology,** 2 (July 1971), 351-368.
8. Gibson, Eleanor, et al. "A Developmental Study of the Discrimination of Letter-Like Forms," **Journal of Comparative and Physiological Psychology,** 55 (December 1962), 897-906.
9. Gibson, James, and Eleanor Gibson. "Perceptual Learning: Differentiation or Enrichment?" **Psychological Review,** 62 (January 1955), 32-41.
10. Kagan, Jerome. "Impulsive and Reflective Children: Significance of Conceptual Tempo," in S. Sapir and A. Nitzburg (Eds.), **Children with Learning Problems.** New York: Brunner/Mazel, 1973, 308-317.
11. Kagan, Jerome. "Reflection-Impulsivity: The Generality and Dynamics of Conceptual Tempo," **Journal of Abnormal Psychology,** 71 (February 1966), 17-24.
12. Kagan, Jerome. "Reflection-Impulsivity and Reading Ability," **Child Development,** 36 (September 1965), 609-628.
13. Kagan, Jerome, Howard Moss, and Irving Sigel. "Psychological Significance of Style of Conceptualization," **Monographs of the Society for Research in Child Development,** 28 (1963), 73-112.
14. Kagan, Jerome, Leslie Pearson, and Lois Welch. "Modifiability of an Impulsive Tempo," **Journal of Educational Psychology,** 57 (December 1966), 359-365.
15. Kagan, Jerome, et al. "Information Processing in the Child: Significance of Analytic and Reflective Attitudes," **Psychological Monographs,** 78 (1964).
16. McKinney, James. "Problem-Solving Strategies in Impulsive and Reflective Second Graders," **Developmental Psychology,** 8 (January 1973), 145.
17. Messer, Stanley. "Reflection-Impulsivity: A Review," unpublished paper, December 1974.
18. Robertson, Donald, and Steward Keeley. "Evaluation of a Mediational Training Program for Impulsive Children by a Multiple Case Study Design," paper presented at American Psychological Association, August 1974.
19. Rosenfield, Sylvia. "The Effect of Perceptual Style on Word Discrimination Ability of Kindergarten Children," unpublished doctoral dissertation, University of Wisconsin, 1967.
20. Santostefano, Sebastiano, Louis Rutledge, and David Randall. "Cognitive Styles and Reading Disability," **Psychology in the Schools,** 2 (January 1965), 57-62.
21. Sulzer, Beth, and G. Roy Mayer. **Behavior Modification Procedures for School Personnel.** Hinsdale, Illinois: Dryden Press, 1972.

22. Williams, Joanna. "New Theories of Reading: What Do They Tell Us?" **Teachers College Record**, 75 (May 1974), 553-561.
23. Witkin, Herman, et al. **Psychological Differentiation**. New York: Wiley, 1962.
24. Wright, John. "Reflection-Impulsivity and Information Processing from Three to Nine Years of Age," paper presented at American Psychological Association, August 1974.

ADDITIONAL SOURCES: INSTRUCTIONAL PURPOSE

Cooper, C. R. and A. R. Petrosky. "A Psycholinguistic View of the Fluent Reading Process," **Journal of Reading**, December 1976, 184-207.

The authors define reading as a psycholinguistic process, drawing on the work of Eleanor Gibson, Kenneth Goodman, Frank Smith, and other researchers. Given the complex nature of reading, they present a remarkably clear definition, together with ten strategies used by fluent readers. Based on their views, the authors describe an instructional program appropriate for students who have achieved basic literacy skills, which they define as at least third grade ability as measured by a standardized elementary reading test.

Singer, H.S., and R.B. Ruddell (Eds.). **Theoretical Models and Processes of Reading** (second edition). Newark, Delaware: International Reading Association, 1976.

This revised edition represents perhaps the most recent and thorough treatment of the subject. Since the reader may risk being overwhelmed by the sheer size of the volume, to say nothing of the complexity of the topic, it is suggested that three of the many articles be studied carefully.

"The Nature of the Reading Process," by J.B. Carroll (pp. 8-18), provides a very readable discussion of mature reading. The author then distinguishes mature reading from the process of learning to read and examines different approaches and sequences in the teaching of reading. The distinction made between reading and learning to read is essential for every teacher of reading.

"Behind the Eye: What Happens in Reading," by K.S. Goodman (pp. 470-496), is a more detailed explanation of language behavior, with emphasis on the author's model of reading. Goodman describes the processing of graphophonic, syntactic, and semantic information in decoding written messages, and translates his definition into instructional objectives and strategies for the reading curriculum.

"The Function of Attitude in the Reading Process," by G.C. Mathewson (pp. 655-676), presents a definition of reading which elaborates on the influence of attitude in the reading process. The author does not claim to fully describe reading behavior. However, his model serves as an interesting exploration of the interrelationships among affective factors, comprehension, and reading achievement. Mathewson also presents possible implications for classroom practice.

MATERIALS

METHODS

INSTRUCTIONAL PURPOSE

MANAGEMENT

Evaluation

The instructional program demands the direct teaching of the skills and processes of reading. The teacher who has formulated a clear instructional purpose knows what to look for as evidence of reader strength and reader need. In the context of diagnostic/prescriptive instruction, therefore, a clear definition of the reading process points the way to the second essential step—formative evaluation. Formative evaluation, also known as pretesting or diagnosis, is the careful observation of each student's behavior in order to determine his/her present status with regard to the skills, styles, attitudes, and other facets of fluent reading.

Even as reading is rarely defined as a single skill, reading status cannot be determined by a single observation. Teachers are aware of any number of observational techniques useful for collecting information about student reading behavior. These range from informal conversation and individual conferences, through group inventories and the cloze procedure, to commercial survey tests and extensive (even computerized) diagnostic batteries. Any technique is useful if it provides direct information on an important component of reading competence.

Formative evaluation, as the name implies, must lead the teacher to decisions which **form** subsequent instruction. Careful examination of the collected information will indicate appropriate prescriptions; that is, materials and methods which match the needs of individuals and groups within the classroom.

This section presents two discussions of formative evaluation. The authors list several ways to observe student strengths and needs and outline the knowledge and skills necessary in implementing an effective diagnostic/prescriptive program. One or more ideas may add to your competence as a diagnostic teacher of reading.

The Reading Teacher as Diagnostician

ALBERT J. HARRIS, Professor Emeritus
City University of New York

For nearly forty years, reading specialists have dreamed of classrooms where each child develops reading ability according to his/her own particular needs. In 1938, Cole (1) described a reading classroom in which a child came in, took an exercise from the files, sat down and worked on it, and then got an answer key and corrected it. When a child finished a series of exercises, the teacher checked his mastery of the skill and then gave him a new assignment. The teacher did little direct teaching but, rather, decided what kinds of practice each child needed, assigned practice materials, checked progress, helped children over trouble spots, and supplied motivation and enthusiasm.

For the most part, this dream failed to catch on. Until the mid sixties, those who advocated individualized reading tended to follow the Willard Olson pattern which stressed seeking, self-selection, and self-pacing. The child looked for reading material, chose it himself, and went through it at his own rate. Skills teaching was not stressed in such individualized classrooms and, while good readers often made excellent progress, the direction and specific help poor readers needed was often lacking.

During the 1960s the tide turned. Research had demonstrated that the laissez-faire type of individualized reading generally produced no better results than the severely criticized basal readers. The development of programed instruction spurred the production of self-teaching, self-marking materials. Attempts were made to apply the systems concept to reading instruction. Newer systems of individualized instruction appeared, in which the emphasis was on the mastery of skills; systems such as Individually Prescribed Instruction, the PLAN System, and the Wisconsin Reading Design. Strang's book, **Diagnostic Teaching of Reading (4)** was published in 1964. Since then, other books stressing a diagnostic approach to reading instruction have appeared, notably those by Guszak (2) and Harris and Smith (3).

Teacher as Diagnostician

Can the teacher of reading be a diagnostician? Yes, if the teacher has the knowledge, facilities, and skills necessary to make diagnostic teaching work. For a truly diagnostic classroom is quite different from the typical classroom of today.

What kind of diagnostician should a classroom teacher of reading be? Not a psychologist or psychiatrist, but a person able to recognize the possibility that a particular child's erratic learning may be due to an emotional disturbance that needs intensive study. Not a neurologist, not an ophthalmologist, not a hearing specialist, but an individual sensitive to the presence of behavior that suggests the desirability of referral for professional examination in one of these areas. The reading teacher should know enough about the causation of reading disabilities to be able to suspect interfering handicaps and to refer students for specialized diagnostic study when necessary. But when it comes to the analysis of the child's reading performance, that is, in determining the skills he needs and how he may best be taught, the reading teacher should be the diagnostician.

Teacher Knowledge

It is possible for a classroom teacher who knows little about reading to follow a basal reader guide and get reasonable results. An effective diagnostic reading teacher, however, needs a comprehensive acquaintance with the objectives of reading instruction. He should be familiar with the specific knowledge and skills to be mastered at many levels of the reading program, and should have detailed lists of these objectives for ready reference. The teacher should understand the difference between outcome objectives and process objectives. The former, often called behavioral, or performance objectives, are formulated in terms of what the child can do once he has mastered the objectives. The latter describes what the teacher can do to help children achieve the outcome objectives.

Second, the teacher needs to be acquainted with the wide variety of materials that may be useful in a diagnostically oriented reading program. These include: basal readers and their guides over a wide range of reading levels, related workbooks, independent workbooks for specific skills, boxed multilevel materials of the kit or laboratory type, audiovisual hardware and software combining recordings with printed materials, and commercially available games, as well as teacher-constructed materials. The teacher also needs to know where to find or how to construct the many criterion-referenced mastery tests needed to evaluate each step of progress.

Finally, the teacher needs an understanding of the steps necessary to begin a diagnostically oriented program and to run it with reasonable effectiveness. In addition to knowledge which can be gained through reading, it is almost essential to have a principal, reading supervisor, or consultant who can help the teacher in the difficult planning stage and help to solve specific problems as they arise.

Resources for the Teacher

In addition to conventional readers and workbooks covering a wide range of reading levels, the diagnostic classroom needs materials which do not require instruction or correction by the teacher. They may include programed materials, self-checking workbooks that use chemically treated paper to show if a response is right or wrong, exercises with answer keys usable by the pupils, exercises with recorded directions and scoring instructions, picture-word and picture-phrase cards, and so on. Stories or whole books can be recorded so that children can read along while they listen. Instruments like the Language Master allow a child to look at a printed word, hear the spoken equivalent, record his own response on another trial, and then compare the two responses. And, of course, every reading classroom should have a library corner. Projection equipment dresses up the room but does not add much to teaching effectiveness.

Materials are not very helpful if the teacher is not systematic. Many hours need to be spent on classifying materials, coding them by type and difficulty level, and filing them so that they are easily accessible to pupils and teachers. More hours are required to prepare and arrange the self-checking tests for pupil use and the mastery tests which the teacher will use. Still more hours must go into developing and maintaining a record-keeping system.

In some systems approaches to reading instruction, the teacher's burden is lightened by provision of machine scoring or computer scoring and recording of test results. This is a doubtful blessing, since counting errors does not tell us why the errors were made. By inspecting the kinds of errors, and by asking the child how he arrived at the responses, the teacher may pinpoint a particular confusion that can be cleared up readily once it is recognized. If one assigns more practice of the same kind, without getting at the nature of the difficulty, the child may get only more practice in making wrong responses and, at the same time, become increasingly discouraged.

Perhaps more than anything else, the diagnostic teacher needs the encouragement and approval of the school principal. With such support, the teacher can hope to assemble enough of the kinds of materials needed to make a diagnostic approach feasible. With proper support, the teacher can forge ahead, reassured that the mistakes of inexperience will not be taken too seriously; he or she can expect support in presenting the idea to parents and colleagues; and chances of getting other teachers to join in are much greater. Without support, the teacher may well conclude that discretion is the better part of valor.

Determining Pupil Needs and Abilities

Although for many years textbooks on the teaching of reading have been explaining the concepts of independent, instructional, and frustration reading levels, some teachers are far from expert in deciding on the proper instructional levels for their pupils. In general, teachers tend not to hear all of the miscues made and they overestimate more often than underestimate the child's instructional level. One needs to sharpen one's perceptions of children's reading efforts. It is an excellent idea to tape the child's reading and to analyze it later in peace and quiet. It is still better if several teachers listen to the same recorded performance, make their independent records and evaluations, and compare. The same is true with oral tests of word recognition and phonic knowledge. If it is not practicable to take a course on reading diagnosis, continuing efforts to record accurately and interpret correctly will usually bring gradual improvement, especially when done with other teachers. When pupils have trouble with a written or objective test, asking them to explain how they got their answers is very rewarding. Perceiving and understanding pupil errors is a subtle combination of teaching skills that cannot be learned all at once.

Organizing the Class

A teacher who wishes to move into diagnostic teaching is well advised to do so one step at a time. A first step might be to relieve the most mature readers of exercises they do not need and allow them to use the time gained for project work or for tutoring classmates with more limited reading ability. Starting with the mature students makes individualization something to be prized and sought. A second step might be to replace around-the-group oral reading by the least mature readers with paired reading. Even when the pairs are buddies with approximately equal reading skills overall, the readers usually do not have trouble with the exact same words. Pairing of most and least mature readers also can be useful. Once the extremes have become accustomed to new procedures, some changes can be made for the remaining children. During the month or two in which these preliminary steps are taken, the teacher should have been working on collecting and organizing materials for individual skills practice and, once these are ready, the most mature group may again lead the way. The differing procedures for practice exercises and tests of mastery may take several explanations. A complete transition to a fully organized diagnostic system could take a year or more.

Record Keeping

The importance of developing and maintaining a record keeping system has already been mentioned. Formulating a comprehensive list of behavioral objectives from teacher guides designed for that purpose can be tedious and very time-consuming. So can the writing of a set of mastery tests for each objective. Fortunately, some publishers of basal readers have begun to provide teachers with lists of objectives book by book and have indicated for each objective a particular workbook or dittoed exercise that can serve as the mastery test for it. Several sets of criterion-based mastery tests are also available commercially.

The teacher's recording system can be made efficient by the extensive use of abbreviations and code symbols. They can be cross-referenced from the behavioral objective to the mastery test and the exercises that go with it. There needs to be room for qualitative comments and descriptive anecdotes, also. A double-page spread will usually take care of the recording needed for one child. In addition, it is helpful to have a master check sheet in which the teacher can record the date when each child accomplishes a specific objective. Not all learning, of course, has to be done individually in a diagnostic classroom. A group with common skill needs can be brought together for instruction in that skill, and then given individualized practice.

The pupil also needs a record of the work he is to do, and of what he has accomplished. This can be worked out a week at a time and can show the stories to be read, words to be learned, decoding principles to be mastered, and comprehension quizzes to be answered. The pupil should have a separate record of independent reading completed.

Motivating

If children are placed at their proper instructional levels and are consistently given things to do which are sufficiently challenging and interesting, but at a level which assures reasonable success, the need for conventional discipline diminishes. All children at every level of ability enjoy having their efforts appreciated, their products praised, and their difficulties treated sympathetically. The diagnostic teacher is the main source of morale for the class as a whole and for each child in it. A pat on the back here, a word of praise there, recognition that a particular task was especially hard, an approving smile—these are vital to the success of a diagnostic teacher.

Summary

The focus of diagnostic teaching is not on causation but on the here and now of what the child can and cannot do, what skills he has and what skills he needs, and on matching this information with appropriate opportunities for learning. The diagnostic teacher must know the scope and sequence of the total reading program. He or she needs to know materials which foster independent learning. He or she requires appropriate materials, a carefully planned system, and support from administrators and supervisors. The diagnostic teacher should be skilled in analyzing pupil needs, in organizing a class for differentiated instruction, in record keeping, and in motivating pupils.

With patience, effort, and desire; with knowledge, skills, and experience; with materials, system, and support, the teacher of reading can become a successful diagnostician.

References

1. Cole, Luella. **The Improvement of Reading**. New York: Farrar and Rinehart, 1938.
2. Guszak, Frank J. **Diagnostic Reading Instruction in the Elementary School.** New York: Harper and Row, 1972.
3. Harris, Larry A., and Carl B. Smith. **Reading Instruction through Diagnostic Teaching.** New York: Holt, Rinehart and Winston, 1972.
4. Strang, Ruth. **Diagnostic Teaching of Reading**. New York: McGraw-Hill, 1964.

Informal Diagnosis: The Nucleus

SAM V. DAUZAT
Louisiana Tech University

For the past decade and a half, the concept of individualized instruction has kept educators in constant turmoil: engaging in discussions, considering possibilities, making varying degrees of commitment, and generally intellectualizing. The philosophizing and theorizing have resulted in too little actualizing. Even though most educators accept the philosophy underlying individualized instruction, particularly for the skills areas of the curriculum, they appear to lack the organizational-management skills necessary to actualize an individualized program. Skill in diagnostic procedures is a prime requisite in implementing individualized instruction. Without such skill, the classroom practitioner can never bridge the gap between theory and practice. Diagnosis must be the pivot point, the basic ingredient in a system which facilitates and supports individualized instruction.

Reading is one area of the curriculum in which there is keen need for individualization of instruction. The very nature of the reading process, with its intricate network of skills, almost demands that an instructional program be based upon the skills needs of the reader or potential reader. Such an instructional program cannot exist in the absence of diagnosis, the results of which must determine program goals and directions, program content, program materials, and organizational procedures. Diagnosis is increasingly becoming the password for effective reading programs at all levels — school system, school, and individual classroom. Because of this, diagnosis must be added to the list of competencies required of the effective classroom teacher of reading. Each teacher must develop the understanding of and skill in applying basic diagnostic techniques which enable her to determine the reading strengths and weaknesses of each member of the class.

Hindering Factors

Despite the recent treatment of reading diagnosis in professional meetings, books, and journals, several factors remain which hinder progress in teacher development and use of effective diagnostic procedures. If the benefits of diagnosis as prerequisite to individualized reading programs are to be realized, these hindering factors must be offset by facilitating forces. Several hindering factors follow, along with their facilitating counterparts.

1. **Hindering.** Traditional views have focused on diagnosis as a negative term and process. Diagnosis has been accepted in the past as something done **to** the reader **by** a reading specialists **in** a private setting **after** the reader had begun to show obvious evidence of reading problems.

   Facilitating. The positive aspects of diagnosis must be stressed. Diagnosis must be understood as the process for determining reading skills of all pupils and as the basis for instructional decisions on goals, methods, materials, and organizational designs.

2. **Hindering.** In traditional views, diagnosis was almost exclusively a highly formal process. The extensive series of tests designed to determine the complex causes of reading disabilities created an aura of mystery about diagnostic procedures which could be solved only by highly trained reading specialists.

   Facilitating. Diagnosis must be expanded to include the informal procedures which the classroom teacher can implement quickly and accurately in the regular classroom setting with all children, not just with those who are experiencing problems. The purposes of informal diagnosis must focus more on the identification of the student's immediate reading needs than on the identification of and causes for a reading problem.

3. **Hindering.** The diagnostic data reported to the teacher were in highly technical jargon. The case reports from the specialist further served to overwhelm the teacher with technicalities and convince her of her inadequacies, not only in applying diagnostic techniques but also in understanding and utilizing diagnostic data to provide more meaningful instruction.

   Facilitating. Informal diagnostic procedures must yield data which can be employed readily in making such instructional decisions as: Which skills must receive high priority for instruction? How should they be sequenced? Which materials are most appropriate? How can the class be organized most effectively?

4. **Hindering.** Usually, only rather limited benefits resulted from the indepth diagnosis. Too frequently, the case report and the detailed diagnostic analysis were the end products and not the means of more meaningful instruction for the child.
   Facilitating. Diagnosis in reading must be viewed as a vehicle through which more meaningful, personalized instruction may be provided for each child in the class. In order for this to be workable, the vehicle must be in operation—constantly shifting gears, changing directions, and changing speeds as dictated by the signals present in the classroom scene.

5. **Hindering.** Too often, diagnosis has been accepted as the exclusive domain and responsibility of a specialist. The teacher refers the child for diagnosis and there her responsibility ends. She and the child just "mark time" in the classroom until the child has his turn for testing in the over-crowded schedule of the diagnostician.
   Facilitating. In order for diagnosis in reading to make a positive contribution for the child, the responsibility for informal diagnosis must be assumed by the classroom teacher. The reading specialist may serve to 1) guide the teacher in the development of competencies in utilizing informal diagnostic procedures and 2) undertake indepth diagnosis of certain reading problems, but the real responsibility for diagnosis on a day-to-day basis must be accepted by the classroom teacher. The success of an individualized developmental program in reading is contingent upon the teacher's acceptance of this role.

It is necessary, then, to consider diagnosis as the domain of the classroom teacher, utilizing informal procedures and providing for every child in the program. In short, continuous diagnosis must become the nucleus of a reading program which caters to the needs of all readers.

It would be unrealistic to expect that the same diagnostic techniques which have proved successful in clinical settings with individual children would be appropriate for classroom use in large group settings without adaptations and revisions. The teacher needs access to rapidly implemented procedures which yield relatively accurate data. The remainder of this paper describes diagnostic procedures which incorporate the facilitating factors mentioned above.

Establishing Reading Levels

One of the significant tasks for the teacher, particularly as she first meets the pupil, is the proper placement of the pupil in instructional materials. There is a grave need for the teacher to identify the level of reading materials at which the child can profit most from instruction—his basal or instructional level. Establishing the basal reading level of the student and providing instructional materials at a level compatible with the child's instructional reading level are the points of departure for the program—a first step. Other steps in the process include observing the child's response to the materials, noting obvious telltale signs of frustration and/or lack of challenge, and making the indicated adjustments in the level of difficulty of the materials.

The classroom teacher usually has access to information concerning the child's performance on standardized reading survey tests. This information may prove useful even though the grade equivalent scores provided by many standardized tests are not reliable indexes of the child's appropriate reading level. **A rough index** of the child's instructional level, which can be used as a beginning point, can be determined by subtracting one year from the child's grade equivalency rating scored on a standardized reading survey test (1). The teacher must supplement the suggested rough index with additional data in making the determination of each child's instructional reading level.

The **cloze technique** may be quickly used to estimate reading levels. The cloze exercise consists of a passage of about 250 words from which every fifth word has been deleted, except for the first and last sentences which remain intact. The student's task is to read the passage and supply the exact deleted item in each case. After scoring a passage with fifty deletions, the child's level can be determined from the following range of correct responses (3).

Level	Percent of Correct Responses
Independent	Above 50
Instructional	Between 40 and 50*
Frustration	40 or below

*Editor's Note: Cloze scores must be interpreted with flexibility. Many teachers find that the instructional level is best represented by scores falling between 35 and 55 percent of correct responses.

An exact determination of the reading levels established by the cloze technique, as compared to those determined by graded oral reading paragraphs on an informal reading inventory, may be made through the following procedure (2).

1. Divide the number of words exactly replaced by the total number of blanks.

2. Multiply this figure by 1.67 to determine the average comprehension.

The teacher must then compare the derived comprehension score with the comprehension criteria for levels established by the given school system. Commonly accepted criteria for the levels are: 1) independent level—at least 99 percent accuracy in word recognition and at least 90 percent average comprehension, 2) instructional level—at least 95 percent accuracy in word recognition and at least 75 percent average comprehension, and 3) frustration level—below 90 percent accuracy in word recognition and below 75 percent average comprehension.

The cloze technique has distinct advantages for the classroom diagnostician since it can be adapted for either individual or whole group use. The teacher may have the child read the cloze exercise onto tape for future analysis.

Oral reading from graded passages also gives the teacher valuable information about the child's reading levels. In order to quickly determine whether the materials are at a level too difficult for the child, the teacher need spend only two or three minutes listening to the child sight read orally a short passage from any material and then noting the word recognition errors the child makes. The previously described criteria for accuracy in word recognition may be used for decision making. Errors to be considered in determining word recognition accuracy include: substitutions, insertions, omissions, reversals, mispronunciations, and refusals to try to say the word. The major concern with the quick oral reading assessment for determining reading levels is the total number of word recognition errors. However, notations of the types of errors offer valuable diagnostic data for analysis of skills needs.

Another quickly administered device for determining approximate instructional levels is the commercially prepared Slosson Oral Reading Test. However, the same procedures can be applied to any graded list of words. Having students read isolated words from the list, and applying criteria for accuracy in word recognition to the students' performances, will yield approximate reading levels.

Determining Reading Skill Needs

Once the teacher knows the instructional reading levels of her students, she must determine the reading skills of importance at each level and diagnose each student for skills needs. **Skill checklists**, or objectives arranged in levels of difficulty, provide valuable possibilities for securing diagnostic data relative to reading skills. The checklist serves to structure the teacher's observation of the child's reading performance in varied settings throughout the school day. Through carefully planned, purposeful observations based on the framework of a well-constructed checklist, the teacher can collect "reality based" data on highly specific aspects of the child's reading skills as well as his reading behaviors in the affective domain.

Pupil response cards, used in a variety of reading settings, can be of immense value as a diagnostic technique. In order to use the technique, the teacher must structure a short exercise which focuses on a highly specific reading skill and which requires responses from the children. For example, in checking the child's skill in distinguishing between the hard and soft sounds of **c**, the teacher can give a list of words illustrating the patterns and have all children respond to each word by holding the appropriate response card, perhaps one colored card representing hard **c** and a different colored card representing soft **c**. The teacher can immediately identify by their color coded responses those children who are proficient in the skill as well as those who need further work. Many reading skills lend themselves to checking by this quick, group oriented diagnostic technique.

Sample products of children's work over a period of time offer valuable data for noting patterns of errors and areas of progress in specific reading skills. Since one principle of diagnosis stresses that diagnostic decisions must never be made on the basis of a single performance, the teacher who utilizes sample products is more likely to make accurate diagnostic interpretations. The sample products can be placed in individual folders, or they can be cataloged in folders according to skills.

Further analysis of the child's performance on the informal assessments for determining reading levels can provide useful data on the child's reading skill needs and proficiencies. 1) The child's performance on cloze exercises provides data on his ability in application of context clues. 2) His oral reading of graded passages can be analyzed for patterns in two skills areas: a) oral reading behaviors and b) word recognition in the major error categories of substitutions, insertions, omissions, mispronunciations, and refusals to try. A pattern of error in any one category can be further analyzed for specifics: types of words, types of sounds, etc. Similar types of specific data can be gleaned from an analysis of the child's oral reading of graded lists of words. 3) Analysis of acceptable standardized reading survey tests for the child's perform- ance on individual items yields data useful in diagnosis. The teacher must ascertain, however, that the actual test items measure a given skill before she attempts to analyze for patterns of strength and weakness.

Criterion referenced inventories can be highly valuable for diagnosis of all reading skills. The criterion referenced test identifies the skills which the child has mastered and those which he has not yet acquired, thereby enabling the teacher to make instructional decisions about specific reading skills. The teacher can quickly prepare criterion referenced inventories for the reading skills of importance in her given classroom. The inventories need not be formal and the previously described pupil response cards may be used in conjunction with the inventories to facilitate rapid decision making.

Utilization of Diagnostic Data

Diagnosis cannot be divorced from prescriptive teaching in reading. As soon as the teacher discovers at least one reading need for each child, she can begin to utilize that information in instructional decision making.

In order for diagnosis to be a preventive as well as a remedial measure, teachers must utilize all diagnostic data relative to reading needs of children to provide immediate instruction to prevent those reading needs from becoming reading problems.

Recording the diagnostic data in manageable forms is most important. One useful method is the group check sheet and/or profile sheet for each skill of concern. On the group profile sheet, the teacher lists in a column the names of the children in the class and identifies the major skill and its subsets of skills. Throughout the day, the teacher may record instances of each child's performance in the skill area. The group profile sheet is particularly useful when utilizing such diagnostic techniques as structured teacher observations, individual response cards, oral reading and sample products, or any combination of these techniques. The information recorded on the group profile sheet can be analyzed quickly to identify children needing specific skills instruction and to group those children for provision of that instruction.

An individual profile sheet of specific skills may be kept for each student; however, it is more difficult and time-consuming for the teacher to record data on individual sheets than on group sheets. Still, an analysis of individual profiles will make it possible for the teacher to identify children with similar patterns of need for grouping purposes.

Summary

If teachers are to bridge the gap between theory and practice in individualizing instructional programs in reading, they must have clear evidence of the various needs of each individual in the classroom. Diagnosis is the means for ascertaining the strengths and weaknesses of each child, not just for those children experiencing reading problems. Individualized reading instruction can be realized when skills in diagnosis are developed and utilized by classroom teachers in ongoing classroom settings.

Various techniques and instruments can be developed and/or adapted for classroom use as the teacher gathers diagnostic data on each child in terms of his reading levels and his reading skills. The informal procedures suggested here are quickly administered and easily interpreted. The resulting diagnostic data can serve to guide the teacher in making instructional decisions about scope and sequence of reading skills, materials to be utilized, and classroom organization—management designs which are essential   to instruction based on individual needs in reading.

References

1. Dallmann, Martha, and others. **The Teaching of Reading**. New York: Holt, Rinehart and Winston, 1974, 409.
2. Miller, Wilma. **Reading Diagnosis Kit.** New York: Center for Applied Research in Education, 1974, 221.
3. Zintz, Miles. **Corrective Reading**. Dubuque, Iowa: Wm. C. Brown, 1972, 48-50.

Dauzat

ADDITIONAL SOURCES: EVALUATION

Barrett, T.C. (Ed.). **Evaluation of Children's Reading Achievement**. Newark, Delaware: International Reading Association, 1967.
This is one of the best collections of articles on evaluation, especially as it lends itself to direct application by the classroom teacher. The various chapters treat evaluation in relation to program goals, survey and diagnostic tests, informal inventories, teacher-pupil conferences, and other useful and interesting topics. Overall, an extremely valuable source.

Ekwall, E. E. **Diagnosis and Remediation of the Disabled Reader**. Boston: Allyn and Bacon, 1976.
One of the most recent treatments of diagnosis and prescription, this book presents an in-depth discussion of reading skills, followed by chapters devoted to specific evaluation and prescription information for each skill area. In addition to detailed explanations of tests and testing techniques specific to each identified reading skill, appendices contain extensive listings of individual and group tests and inventories.

Goodman, Y. M. and C. L. Burke. **Reading Miscue Inventory Manual**. New York: Macmillan, 1972.
This manual, which accompanies the complete kit, offers the teacher a clear explanation of the reading process, the use of the inventory to record graphophonic, syntactic, and semantic reader errors, and various instructional strategies for use with readers who exhibit differing miscue patterns. Although the teacher is not likely to use this means of evaluation with all students in the classroom, the insight to be gained from this source should be invaluable in implementing any approach to diagnostic/prescriptive instruction. Perhaps the two most important understandings to be derived are 1) the necessity of noting reader strengths as well as weaknesses, and 2) the realization that there is a very real qualitative difference among types of reader "errors."

Jones, M. B., and E. B. Pikulski. "Cloze for the Classroom," **Journal of Reading**, March 1974, 432-438.
The authors report the results of a comparison among three means of determining appropriate pupil placement in reading materials: the informal reading inventory, the cloze procedure, and a standardized reading test. The use of the cloze procedure in a sixth grade classroom is explained in detail. In addition, teachers should find the discussion of the advantages and limitations of the three methods useful in planning classroom evaluation.

Johnson, M. S., and R. A. Kress. **Informal Reading Inventories**. Newark, Delaware: International Reading Association, 1965.
This all-time IRA best seller remains a most useful reading aid for teachers in evaluating reading performance. The authors provide specific directions for constructing and using informal devices for evaluation. In addition, for the careful reader, they demonstrate basic tenets of sound instructional procedures which are applicable to individual and classroom instruction.

Materials

Having determined the present status of each student insofar as possible, the classroom teacher now seeks instructional materials which 1) represent appropriate levels of difficulty, 2) reflect student interests as well as student needs, and 3) serve as vehicles for exploration and explanation of one or more facets of the reading process. These criteria are applied to instructional materials with specific individuals or subgroups of students in mind, always based on the strengths and/or needs revealed by the formative evaluation.

There are at least five sources of instructional materials in reading.

1. Published materials designed expressly for that purpose (basal readers, kits, workbooks, and skill builders)
2. Published materials not designed for reading skill instruction (newspapers, newsmagazines, and trade books)
3. Materials (usually free) designed to promote, guide, or explain (road maps, promotional brochures, driver manuals, political handouts)
4. Teacher-made materials (flash cards, games, stories, adaptions of published material)
5. Student talk, recorded or dictated and then transcribed (original stories or poems, graffiti, class magazines or newspapers)

Of a seemingly infinite number of specific instructional materials represented by the above categories, this section presents four ideas to add to your perspective.

Word Lists that Make Sense

DALE D. JOHNSON
University of Wisconsin

I still hold the somewhat old-fashioned conviction that written words are important in reading. I realize it is more fashionable to be concerned with syntactic structures, semantic nuances, and phonological relationships as important planks in bridging the gap from printed surface structure to the writer's or reader's deep structures; and I agree that they are important. Yet without **words,** they are meaningless.

Syntactic structures—patterned, diagramed, formulized, or described—are useless without words. The formula "Article + Subject + Auxiliary + Verb + Article + Direct Object," is of no use to a reader until the words, "The boy can drive the car." have been inserted.

Similarly, letter-sound correspondences, arrangements, and sequences—be they labeled rules, spelling patterns, decoding patterns, graphemic bases, phonograms, or whatever—have no utility except in the context of words. We may wish to call words morphemes or free morphemes or word-length units of meaning (as one test does) but, however labeled, they are inescapably important components of language which, in their written forms, must be dealt with by readers.

Types of Word Lists

With this brief statement of bias as an introduction, I wish to use the remaining space discussing things I think are important (or unimportant) about word lists. For many decades, reading teachers and researchers have been compiling lists of words they feel are useful. For example, while at a small college in Wisconsin, Cameron (1) tabulated the profanity of undergraduate students as overheard in dormitories, hallways, and campus taverns. In analyzing his results, Cameron neatly categorized such words according to their derivation: sacred, excretory, or sexual. From a different direction, Hill (6) compiled words found in best-selling comic books during World War II. Davis (4) prepared a list of what he termed "indispensable words" (such as bus stop, exit, toilet) common to everyday environment. Such lists are no doubt interesting and, in some cases, may be useful to young readers.

Obviously, there are many purposes for and potential uses of word lists. Teachers of English as a second language may desire lists of words considered important to the oral language development of non-English speaking children. Researchers may require lists of CVC trigrams or tallies of homographs or homophones. Struggling textbook and test authors may wish for lists of picturable words or words common to a particular discipline. Spelling reformers like lists of words which demonstrate the peculiarities of English spelling, while phonics advocates search for clusters of words that end in **tch** or **ght** or contain the /ɔ/ sound of **o** in medial position.

Our concern in this paper is with vocabularies for beginning reading. We are asking the question, "What kinds of words, that is, which words do we consider important for young children to learn to read?" Certainly, one's philosophy of what beginning reading should be determines the important criteria. In fact, it is possible to categorize neatly the major approaches to beginning reading, as well as many commercially produced reading series, according to their beliefs about "first words"—the initial reading vocabulary.

Those of us who advocate organic reading, the language experience approach, believe that children should be allowed to choose the words they want to learn to read. Those who believe in the importance of decoding in initial reading want to see first words which are consistent and patterned with regard to letter-sound correspondences. Proponents of what we might collectively call "a basal reader" approach see the need for teaching high frequency words—those words children will likely run into over and over again.

Nonetheless, through the years, many teachers of reading have felt a need for what may be called "a basic sight word list." That is, teachers would like a list of words considered vitally important for their pupils to know, regardless of underlying reading philosophy. And reading researchers have tried to meet these needs. In this decade, alone, more than one hundred word lists—some very short and some very comprehensive—have appeared in the literature. Over 3,000 references are cited in the revised **Bibliography of Vocabulary Studies** by Dale, Razik, and Petty (**3**). Some lists seem to have been more soundly derived than others. However, if we look at the scores of lists based on some sort of frequency count and then look at the one hundred or more most frequently listed words, most of the lists look a lot alike.

I wish to suggest to you four postulates or canons which I believe should guide the construction of word lists and the subsequent related teaching, writing, and research.

Changing Language

The first canon is that no word list should be considered sacred, universally useful, or final. Language changes constantly and new words enter a language daily.

Some words mean one thing today and another thing tomorrow. We could play a game we might call "Generation Gap." As you read each of the following words, think of a word or two—perhaps a synonym or a definition—which the word brings to mind: **pot, salt, heavy, Apollo, bag, plumbers.**

Just as some words change in meaning, others fade in usage. Words, such as **shall, pshaw,** and **gully,** once may have been useful to learn but today are much less useful. A word list compiled in the twenties may contain a number of words which are relatively less important in the seventies. Lists compiled today will certainly need regular reevaluation in the future.

Children's Usage

My second canon of word list compilation is that such lists must be based on the language of children. Unless initial reading vocabularies contain words which are in the speaking and listening vocabularies of young children, they cannot be very meaningful. Pioneer work such as that done by Horn (**7**) in 1926, the International Kindergarten Union (**8**) in 1928, Rinsland (**12**) in 1945, and more recent works by Murphy (**11**) in 1957, Wepman and Hass (**14**) in 1969, and Sherk (**13**) in 1973 are studies generated from the oral speech of young children. These studies are quite massive and, because they present the words used by young children from various milieu, should certainly be valuable sources for compiling the usually shorter sight-word lists used in reading.

Comprehensive Sample

A third canon is that, in addition to containing words known by children, beginning word lists should reflect the present day world of printed American English in **all** its genre. By this I mean that the vast array of general printed matter, as well as children's literature, should be a basic source of sight-word vocabulary. Please note that I have not included basal readers.

In my opinion, the dozens of studies compiling words found in basal reading series have been the most uninteresting and the most unproductive form of vocabulary research. There are two main problems with such studies. The reasoning behind them has often been illogical and, certainly, circular. Of what use is it to compile lists of 100 words or 400 words common to eight out of ten basic reading series? Is any child taught to read with this wide array of basal series? Only in the wealthiest of school districts are more than two or three series purchased, and then they are usually intended for rather discrete groups of children. I have nothing against teaching children the new vocabulary they will encounter in their reading book; I think it is imperative, and I am happy that most basal series are carefully constructed to insure the learning of their vocabularies through a variety of techniques. But it seems senseless to teach a word simply because it is found in six or eight controlled vocabulary basal series.

There is further criticism of vocabularies derived from basal series—their inherent circularity and stagnation. Some popular word lists published thirty or forty years ago were derived from basic reading series then in use. Because of their popularity, such lists became vocabulary sources for a new generation of text authors. Then new lists were pulled from the new basals, and so it goes. I would much rather see the dog wag the tail than the tail wag the dog. It seems to me that instructional reading materials written for children should contain words readers will run into time and again in children's books and magazines and the broader world of printed English newspapers, books, and magazines.

We know that many children read more than their school reading books, and it seems that many other children would read more if they knew the words used in nonschool materials. I argue that, in addition to being taught the words in the reading series in use in the classroom, children should be taught a vocabulary of words they will encounter frequently elsewhere. Of course, there will be overlap between the two.

Two recent studies, facilitated by the use of computer technology, have provided massive lists of words derived solely from textbooks written for children. Harris and Jacobson (5) examined six basal reading series from grades one to six and (commendably) also included two series each in social studies, English, math, and science. They present a core list of words found in at least three of the six basal reading series. The 1971 computer aided compilation by Carroll, Davies, and Richman (2) is more useful in that it sampled magazines, novels, poetry, and general nonfiction in addition to basic textbooks. However, it covered only materials intended for children in grades three through nine.

Three recent compilations provide very useful vocabulary sources for beginning word lists: the 1967 Kucera-Francis (9) study of 50,406 distinct words from more than one million running words found in five hundred 2,000-word samples drawn from fifteen different genres including fiction and the sports page. These words, particularly the top 500 or so, are the words most often found in printed American English. Thus, it would seem imperative for teachers and reading textbook authors to utilize these top words, particularly those words that are also within the speaking-listening vocabularies of young children.

Another potentially valuable source from which basic sight words could be drawn is the 1973 compilation presented by Moe (10), based on his computer analysis of 110 children's books—without controlled vocabularies—which were award winners or runners up in such contests as the Caldecott and the Book World Children's Spring Festival. His list of 200 high frequency words accounted for 61 percent of the more than 100,000 running words. As with the top Kucera-Francis 500, these words should be a valuable source to teachers and authors.

Eighty popular children's library books were computer analyzed by Durr (15) and, from a total of more than 105,000 running words, he presents the 188 words of highest frequency.

High frequency words from studies by Kucera-Francis, Moe, and Durr, which also occur with high frequency in the oral language of children as identified in studies by Murphy, Wepman and Hass, and Sherk, ought to be viewed as the currently most useful words from which to prepare sight word lists for teachers and authors.

Multiple Meanings

A final point concerns the meanings of words found in word lists. Too many sight word lists contain only the printed word with no description of its function or meaning. For example, on Moe's list we see words such as **can, saw,** and **head** while on Durr's list we find **like, right,** and run. Using **run** as an example, we do not know if it equates to fast jogging, a hole in a stocking, water pouring from a tap, an attempt to be elected, a baseball score, or operating a business. Should we advise teachers to check a dictionary and teach the meaning listed first? Should we urge that all meanings for a word be taught? Or should we indicate usage which we are presumably saying is so highly frequent? "My **back** is in **back** of my chest and I rarely take **back** what I've said about how poorly he **backs** up his car." But to quickly **back** off this issue, I suggest that as we feed print into computers we should also provide sufficient instructions to the computer so that the resulting compilations tell us which word meanings we really are advocating.

Summary

Word lists have been around a long time, and will continue to be. The use of computers has greatly facilitated the ease and accuracy of word tabulation, but the lists will be only as language-reflective as the sources from which they are derived. Any list of basic sight words not derived from the language of children and high frequency in general printed English or children's literature beyond basal readers (with their controlled vocabularies) should be viewed suspiciously. Let's not put the cart before the horse. Let's let the language of children and the world of printed English dictate the reading vocabularies to be learned by children and to be found in instructional reading materials, rather than the reverse.

References

1. Cameron, P. "The Language of College Students or Damn All Over," unpublished monograph, Stout State College, Menominee, Wisconsin, 1967.
2. Carroll, J. B., P. Davies, and B. Richman. **American Heritage Word Frequency Book**. Boston: Houghton Mifflin, 1971.
3. Dale, E., T. Razik, and D. Petty. **Bibliography of Vocabulary Studies** (fifth edition). Columbus: Ohio State University, 1973.
4. Davis, D. C. "An Indispensible Sight-Word Vocabulary," unpublished monograph, University of Wisconsin at Madison, 1969.
5. Harris, A.J., and M.D. Jacobson. **Basic Elementary Reading Vocabularies.** New York: Macmillan, 1972.
6. Hill, G. E. "The Vocabulary of Comic Strips," **Journal of Educational Psychology**, 34 (February 1943), 77-87.
7. Horn, E. **A Basic Writing Vocabulary**, University of Iowa Monographs in Education, Series 1, No. 4, 1926.
8. International Kindergarten Union, Child Study Committee. **A Study of the Vocabulary of Children Before Entering the First Grade**. Washington, D.C.: International Kindergarten Union, 1928.
9. Kucera, H., and W. N. Francis. **Computational Analysis of Present Day American English**. Providence, Rhode Island: Brown University Press, 1967.
10. Moe, A. J. "Word Lists for Beginning Readers," **Reading Improvement**, 10 (1973), 11-15.
11. Murphy, H., and others. "The Spontaneous Speaking Vocabulary of Children in Primary Grades," **Journal of Education**, 140 (December 1957), 3-106.
12. Rinsland, H. **A Basic Vocabulary of Elementary School Children**. New York: Macmillan, 1945.
13. Sherk, J. K. **A Word Count of Spoken English of Culturally Disadvantaged Preschool and Elementary Pupils**. Kansas City: University of Missouri, 1973.
14. Wepman, J. M., and W. Hass. **A Spoken Word Count** (Children ages five, six, and seven.). Chicago: Language Research Associates, 1969.
15. Durr, W. K. "Computer Study of High Frequency Words in Popular Trade Juveniles," **Reading Teacher**, 27 (October 1973), 37-42.

Learning to Read
Can Become "Fun and Games"

SUSAN M. GLAZER
Rider College

Most teachers separate work from play and learning from fun in the classroom. A statement often heard by children is "When you finish reading, you may have recess." If one asks a child the difference between work and play, responses may be, "Work is icky, but I do it so that I can play a game." or "I love games but not work." It is time for teachers to bring together in the classroom work, play, learning, and fun. Most reading and language skills can be learned through "gaming." It is not difficult to combine work and play in activities that "turn kids on to reading."

Games fit into two general categories: process games and reinforcement games.

Process Games

Process games teach. When children interact with process activities, they are discovering, experimenting, exploring, and deciding. Because process games are designed to teach (not test), all responses offered by children are correct. These games are error-free. They elicit responses in such a way that children can call on their resources of experience and relate new ideas to ones already internalized. Children should be able to think when manipulating these error-free materials. Thinking is imagining, criticizing, interpreting, hypothesizing, assuming, comparing, and classifying to reach a decision.

When children perform the activities and games that are error-free, they are involved in continuous actions. These actions result in a series of changes in behavior. Such changes are the result of learning by involvement. Our goal as teachers is to help children change their behavior and incorporate newly learned skills into their repertoire of achievements.

In summary, process games must possess the following characteristics. They must 1) develop new ideas based on old ideas; 2) present many solutions to the challenges set by the activities; and 3) be error-free, that is, every response offered by the children is acceptable.

If the activities are truly process oriented, they will automatically insure student success and develop self-confidence. Self-confidence leads to good feelings about learning and to the desire to learn still more.

Reinforcement Games

A reinforcement game strengthens and supports what the child has previously learned. It is different from a process game because there is a correct and an incorrect response. A reinforcement game should increase the child's confidence with a particular skill or content material. In essence, it is a test. If the child has learned the skill or new content, he will respond correctly.

Reinforcement games can be used as both diagnostic and evaluative tools. To diagnose, one can watch a child play a reinforcement game and observe his responses. His responses will indicate his weaknesses and strengths and thus provide the teacher with a measure of his learning. To evaluate, one must ascertain if the goals which were set for learning have been met. Here, too, if the child responds with the appropriate answer, it is an indication of success.

Reinforcement games, therefore, should possess the following characteristics. They should 1) signal one correct response; 2) create competitive situations and perhaps foster team competition; and 3) create feelings of great satisfaction as the child selects the correct response. The following sections contain examples of process and reinforcement games.

PROCESS GAMES FOR WRITING*
The purpose of these games is to encourage children to see and manipulate language in written form.

THE REBUS-CARD ACTIVITY
Materials Needed

tag board	magic markers
old magazines and workbooks	scissors
clear Contact paper	a shoe box
rubber cement	

Constructing the Game
1. Cut out pictures of people, animals, or anything that may fill the noun phrase position in a sentence.
2. Paste them onto tag board that has been cut into 4"x4" squares.
3. On a separate group of 4"x4" square cards, write the following kinds of words: nouns, verbs, adjectives, adverbs, structure words.

---

*The games described on these pages were constructed or adapted for use with children in a laboratory experience by Gail Garber Cohen and Nina Marco, students at Rider College.

4. Cover all cards with clear Contact paper. This will protect the game for long life.
5. Put all cards into a shoe box or a similar container that has been attractively decorated.
6. Put the box on a game table with the following directions:
   Take a picture card.
   Take some word cards.
   Make a sentence.
   Make two sentences.
   Make a story with your sentences.
   Copy your story, if you want to.

THE BLOCK GAME

Materials Needed
2"x2" blocks of wood, 10 inches long. (To begin, 30 blocks are sufficient.)
Glossy paint in red, yellow, blue, purple, white, black, and orange.
Sandpaper.
A big barrel covered with fancy print Contact paper.

Constructing the Game
1. Divide the blocks into seven groups. Sand the wood and paint each group of blocks a different color.
2. Let the paint dry. Designate a color group to each part of speech. The following breakdown might be used:
   red—nouns (boys, girls, dog)
   yellow—verbs (running, is, goes, cuts)
   blue—adjectives (fat, silly)
   purple—adverbs (extremely, quickly)
   orange—(all structure words, predeterminers, etc.)
3. On four sides of each block, write in black paint different words of the appropriate part of speech. (The blank ends of each block are placed together for making sentences.)
4. Put all the blocks into the barrel.
5. The following directions for children should be fastened to the barrel:
   •Take a red block and a yellow block.
   •Make a sentence.
   (Change instructions periodically to encourage children to make more complex sentences.)

THE BALLOON GAME

Materials Needed
paper strips ½" x 4"
pen, crayon, or pencil
balloons

Constructing the Game

1. On each slip of paper write an imaginary fun situation. Examples, follow:
   "You are a reporter on TV You have to advertise peanut butter. What would you say? Write it down."
   "You are a pair of shoes that are worn out. How would you feel if your owner wanted to throw you away? Write it down."
2. Insert messages into balloons.
3. Put all balloons into a box.

Directions to Children

- Select a balloon and blow it up.
- Pop the balloon.
- Read the message inside. Do what it says.

This game provides noisy fun for groups as well as individual children.

REINFORCEMENT GAMES FOR WRITING

Writing endeavors should be corrected for spelling, handwriting, and other mechanical and grammatical skills only when there is a "real" reason. Such reasons for correct writing include:

1. Writing a story for publication in the class newspaper or the school or classroom library.
2. Writing a letter.
3. Writing posters and charts for display purposes.

These kinds of "correct" writing activities should come only after the child feels free to write, without reservation, what he thinks, feels, and knows. For example, the teacher might place on a table some activity cards similar to the following:

Write a story about your family. Have it edited by your teachers or a classmate. Rewrite the story, making the corrections your editors have suggested.

PROCESS GAME FOR COMPOUND WORDS

The purpose of the following activity is to teach a child to create and manipulate compound words.

Materials needed

tag board (cut into 4"x4" squares)
magazines and workbooks
clear Contact paper
magic markers or crayons
scissors

Constructing the Game

1. Cut and paste pictures from printed materials or draw pictures on cards. Be sure that most of the pictures can be combined to form compound words.

2. On the back of each card, print the name of the object shown. Write the word in the middle of the card, being sure that the first and last letters extend as close to the edge of the card as possible.
3. Cover each card with clear Contact paper. The following are suggestions:

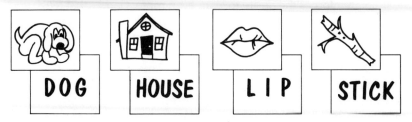

Directions
- Ask the child to put two pictures together. Have him name the two objects from left to right.
- Ask the child to explain the new combination.
- Ask the child to continue this activity, saying the name of the two objects each time another combination is made.
- When the child comes upon a compound word and reads it (i.e., dog and house make doghouse), ask him to draw the object. For example:

- When the child is able to construct a new object from the picture joining activity, turn the cards over and join the words. Then tell the child that he has made a compound word.
- Ask him to tell you what he thinks a compound word is.
- If the child answers correctly, he has gained the concept; if he answers incorrectly, he should repeat the activity.

REINFORCEMENT GAME FOR COMPOUND WORDS
Materials needed
    Use the same materials as required for the process game, but reverse the process activity to test and evaluate learning.
Directions
- Show the child the word and ask him to draw the object it represents.
- Ask what two objects he thinks of when he sees the word.
- Ask the child to draw these two objects.

Summary

If play is the work of the child, games can promote success in learning to read by stimulating a love for language. The resulting success in learning reinforces the desire to learn even more. Games that teach and test can foster both independence and team cooperation by encouraging self-selection, adherence to rules, and awareness of the interests and abilities of individuals and groups. Process and reinforcement games help children develop attitudes of self-assessment by requiring decision making in active, competitive, and purposeful ways. Games that are durable, easy to use, and self-explanatory provide many opportunities for diagnosis, teaching, and evaluation. Most of all, they help children to discover that learning can be fun!

Motivating Reading through Classroom Publications

INEZ MARIE WARE
State University College at Buffalo

All was quiet in the classroom except for the rustle of turning pages as the group of intermediate grade children read intently. "Talk about reading motivation!" exclaimed the teacher.

Previously, reading had not been so enthusiastically pursued by every member of this class. What was the motivating ingredient?

These children now were reading their own magazine—one that they themselves had planned, written, and published—all about animals, a favorite topic of the group. The class had collected newspaper articles and read other information about animals. Each person produced his own ditto master of his story and a picture (some using as many as five colors). Now that the magazine was published, each child could read what he and his friends had written.

Motivation for reading is intrinsic in classroom prepared magazines and newspapers because the material is written by the child himself, the content is relevant to the child's experiences, and the language is the style the child uses. Everyone likes to see his name in print or read a story he has written himself. Children are no exception. Publications thus go one step beyond the motivation inherent in the language experience approach because the child's writing is preserved in a more enduring form.

Classroom publications offer an opportunity for the child to write about his own experiences; in addition the child is exposed to various forms of creative writing that will appear in the class magazine. For example, if the class decides to publish **Haiku Happenings**, the activity provides a pretty good reason for the child to familiarize himself with this type of poetry. In class preparation of newspapers, the child learns techniques for producing various forms of content used in newspapers. In the process, the pupil develops and improves his writing skills in a natural setting and with a purpose in mind.

Above all, the child enhances his self-concept, develops creativity, gains a free time pursuit, and acquires a knowledge of the practical use of research skills needed for some forms of writing.

One fifth grade boy who was not too popular with his peers began work on the class newspaper. Soon, he became interested in making up fictitious ads and showed a flair for this type of writing. As a result, he became advertising manager when the class opened a school store; eventually, his school work, attitude, and popularity showed marked improvement.

Initiation

To motivate interest in publishing, children should visit a local newspaper or print shop, study their local newspaper, and finally produce one of their own design. One teacher sparked interest by making up a newspaper that related to class activities and contained at least one reference to each child in the class. Instead of a name, a series of question marks appeared across the top of the front page. Pupils were invited to name the class paper and then were urged to write one of their own. The motivated class proceeded to do so that very day!

Themes for publications vary. They could relate to the season or a specific holiday; they could be correlated with some content or special interest area. They could be fact or fiction. The reporting could concern current, historic, or futuristic events and be written as if the authors were living in the era described. One class published a newspaper reporting their town's centennial and the children wrote as if they were living and reporting during the earlier time. Pupils rubbed yellow chalk around the edges of the newspaper to make it look old. Town newspaper files were researched for topics to report and long time citizens were interviewed. A feature story revealed that there were not enough older citizens to meet the needs for interviews, so one enterprising person copied names from tombstones in the local cemetery and created stories.

Publication names should be chosen by the full class. Newspapers usually have short titles due to space limitations. Magazines often devote a large portion of their covers to the magazine name and, therefore, can accommodate longer titles. Children should be encouraged to create interesting titles, such as **Smith's Special** (after name of school or teacher), **Cave Man Chronicle, Tales from the Haunted House, Poetry Parade, Moon Tune, Dinosaur Diggings,** or **April Fooler.** Publication themes often can be developed into interesting titles.

As many children as possible should be on the publication staff, especially in the case of newspapers, so that the children's names can thereby appear in print. Some groups manage to include every child's name in an extensive list of positions, such as illustrator, assistant illustrator, reporter, copyeditor, editor, managing editor, proofreader, etc.

Content and Style

Magazine content should be determined and then related to a central theme. This could result in a publication with only one type of writing, such as haiku, tall tales, or mystery stories. Or writing style might be varied but the themes be related (such as stories, poems, and riddles about St. Patrick's Day, or about winter, or **All about Me**).

Newspaper content can be determined by examining a commercial paper or simply by having children suggest what they want to include. Typical content involves news; sports; interviews; roving reporter items; weather; editorials; advice columns; book, movie, record, and TV program reviews; letters to the editor; and advertisements. Content will probably vary according to grade level. Older children might prefer to write about automobiles, fashions, or popular musical groups. Younger children may prefer to report on family or pet activities.

A single article can be done by one child, several in a group, or perhaps by the entire class. At any rate, a deadline should be established and maintained. Some students may not assume responsibility easily; however, once their contributions have been omitted because they were late, these children often are the ones who ask, "When is the next publication coming out?"

Should children's writing be edited or published as written? Opinion differs in regard to corrections of material. Most teachers do stress proofreading by the writer and corrections when necessary for readability. School and grade level standards are usually imposed. It is helpful if editing can be done in consultation with the writer so he can see that the mechanics he studied in class are applied and are useful. Some censorship may be necessary if material is written in poor taste or is perhaps erroneous (these publications do go home to parents). One writer of an advice column, for example, received an inquiry about what to do regarding an annoying brother. The columnist's first suggestion was to "hit him over the head!"

In regard to newspapers, children above the primary level can be instructed in techniques for writing various content. For example, a news story should supply important information first by answering who, what, when, where, and why. News reporters should use short sentences to provide facts; they should avoid giving opinions. An editorial provides the opportunity for voicing opinion and should state a problem or situation and offer suggestions for a solution.

Ads can be realistic (such as publicity about an Open House, a coming assembly, the school store, or lost and found items). On the other hand, fictional ads can be amusing. Children can make up a product, such as Ultra Blight toothpaste, Sugar Hops cereal, Glue hair spray, or Gurgle baby food. Another idea is to base ads on propaganda techniques such as bandwagons, testimonials, and generalizations. Such ads might read: "Are you the only student in class who doesn't have an Answer-Right pen?" "Cinderella uses an Answer-Right pen." or "Get to the top of the class with an Answer-Right pen."

Material should not be limited to school situations. Some schools may have little sports news, for example, so the sports section may include out-of-school interests. Editorials can be based on issues not originating in school but about which children are concerned.

Publication and Layout

The publication process comes after material has been collected. Very few schools below the high school level have print shops, so other forms of duplication are necessary, depending on how many copies are needed. The most popular process is ditto, since it is available in most schools and is easy to use. Ditto masters come in several colors and, thus, add attractiveness to each page.

If the publication is typed, it can be done by the teacher, school secretary, parents, or students, depending on individual skills. Try to avoid a situation similar to one created when a boy in one class volunteered to type at home. When the resulting typed copy was unacceptable, the volunteer typist confessed that he had attempted to use a toy typewriter.

Lengthy magazines should have a cover, title page (containing name and location of school, class grade level, teacher and staff names), and table of contents. Newspapers look better if they have a border line around the outside of each page. This keeps the reader's eye, as well as the typist's lines, from running off the page. Lines also can be drawn between stories to separate items and add graphic interest to the page.

Pictures are a must to break up the monotony and to add attractiveness to the written material. Children who do not turn in written contributions can still be part of the staff by providing illustrations of all sorts. Overlays provide variation; with this technique, a picture is drawn in one color and the writing appears in another color.

Perhaps the most personal aspect of publication comes when the children share in the production process. For example, a group of "class secretaries" can produce the ditto masters or individual children might make their own. It matters little whether the final product wins a prize; more important is that the children share a never to be forgotten experience. To achieve such learning experiences, the class needs specific instruction in procedures. Some children forget to remove the protective paper between the cover and carbon and others think that if they make a mistake on the cover, all they have to do is erase it. One child, thinking everything would come out backwards, drew the American flag in reverse.

If the publication is written, it is best done in manuscript, since this resembles print in commercial publications. Handwriting guidelines for alignment purposes can be drawn with the carbon removed.

After the publication is "printed," children can collate, staple, and distribute. Administrators and teachers of other classes at the same grade level should receive copies. Some groups even send copies to the the Superintendent of Schools.

Necessary Reading Skills

Not only will children want to read their publications, but the reading and writing processes help develop skills of silent and oral reading. Silent reading is smoother and faster because word recognition difficulties are reduced when vocabulary is on the child's experience level. Sentences are structured in familiar patterns in these class written publications.

Comprehension and interpretation skills are promoted in the writing and reading process. Examples are:

Getting the main idea—headlines and titles, opening paragraphs, news stories

Making judgments—editorials, advertisements, columns, reviews

Identifying character traits—interviews, stories, reviews

Promoting creative thinking—all forms of creative writing, advertisements, illustrations

Distinguishing fact from opinion—news stories, editorials, advice columns, reviews, factual stories

Sequence—news stories, creative writing, directions

The reader not only uses and develops comprehension and word recognition skills but study skills, such as skimming and locating information, are necessary. Tables of content, headlines, and pictures are useful here.

In writing based on research, authors may read from various sources; select relevant information; use supporting details; perceive cause-effect relationships, sequence, comparison, and contrast; and draw conclusions. Basing publications on content areas such as social studies and science will lead to such research. One sixth grade class, for example, published **Greek Times**. They wrote articles about Socrates,

Poseidon, customs, gods, olympic games, fashions, and entertainment.

Publications provide natural oral reading situations. There are purposes for reading—to share, inform, and entertain. Since material is familiar because it was self-authored and not copied, the reading is more likely to be fluent and expressive. Some children share their writings with other classrooms, especially on the primary level. Audience interest will be high because they know the authors.

One group of boys, for example, wrote a play called "Santa's Magic Pool Table" for their class publication, **Zippy, Zappy Noel Anthology.** The play was impossible to stage but made a good audience reading situation for the authors. The staging difficulty was due to the plot. Santa received a pool table from Marvel the Magician who neglected to tell Santa that every time he said "Nine," the table would disappear and would reappear when Santa laughed, "Ho, ho, ho!" Naturally, the table keeps popping in and out during the play.

Conclusion

Classroom publications can motivate reading because they offer new experiences for many children. Very little has been done in this area in most classrooms and, as yet, the technique's potential is unreached. One child summed up her publications experience by stating, "We learned a lot of new things. We learned that reading is fun."

Reading that Makes a Difference

FEHL SHIRLEY
California State University at Northridge

"Survival literacy" depends upon the development of humanizing attitudes and behavior toward other living organisms. Humanizing attitudes enable an individual to "let go" of selfish, fear-ridden anxieties and trust the conscience within the self. Self-respect and its correlate, respect for others, can bring about the integration of personality which should be a goal of reading as it is of education in general.

Competency and flexibility in reading skills are subgoals along a development continuum extending from initial language acquisition to the humane being.

The vast and varied field of literature is the essential vehicle in this development. Taught to identify with characters and situations in books, students can achieve insight into the motives and consequences of decisions, thus developing maturity and compassion. If the processes of reading and valuing are related, with unceasing analysis of individual choices in the light of traditional values, students are likely to achieve the ultimate goal—autonomous regulation and altruistic behavior.

Reading and Human Values

Self-regulation and actualization, then, are the goals. A wide range of literature serves as the vehicle. The processes of reading and valuing are the enablers that make a difference in a reading program. The four phases in the program are listed below and are described in detail throughout the remainder of this paper.

1. Finding out where the student is—needs, interests, concerns, and problems.
2. Selecting reading materials in accordance with student needs and concerns.
3. Integrating the processes of reading and valuing through the discussion of literature.
4. Finding out where the teacher is—needs, values, and philosophy of education.

Finding Out Where the Student Is—
Interests, Concerns and Problems

Let us examine briefly three of the many problems and concerns faced by students. One such concern is exemplified in the logic of TV commercials. Advertisers subtly suggest immediate rewards of love, marriage, friends, and prestige as possible results of using their products. Long-term educational goals and perseverance in a task cannot compete with the appeal of material gratifications **now**, particularly for the immature or underprivileged individual. Where is the student on a continuum which ranges from the traditional morality of constraint to the hedonistic principle of immediate gratification?

As the individual matures, another problem arises—the credibility gap between parent and child. Adolescents are sensitive to the discrepancy between principle and practice. They observe that ethical principles often are ignored in the practice of business, government, and sports. Respect for others too often is replaced by competition and winning at all costs, regardless of the means. As the credibility gap widens, the conflict increases between peer values and adult expectation. Where is the student in his attempts to resolve this problem?

The individual also is exposed to violence of two kinds: 1) the outer, historical violence of a possible nuclear holocaust and 2) the psychological violence of sadism, exploitation, and aggression, which is difficult to control **(2)**. Perhaps never before have children internalized so many varied ways to commit crimes and exploit human beings. Where is the child in his efforts to rechannel or sublimate destructive thoughts and energies? Where is the child on the continuum from destruction to the preservation of life?

Listening to children can reveal many concerns:

I don't like the way I act.
Some people hate me. I hate myself.

My father lost his job.

My father has a dark complexion.
He's a gardener.

My mother is too busy to help me.

My brother picks on me and gets me into trouble.

I wish I were dead.

The above anxieties of children were noted by tutors who participated in a reading practicum in two elementary schools as part of a preservice reading methods course. In addition to listening and observing, various ways were used to identify the needs and concerns of the children:

Sentence completion inventories.

Drawings—"Me," "What School is Like," "What I Would Like School to Be," "My Home," "My Family."

Autobiographies—"The Kind of a Person I Think I Am," "The Kind of Person Others Think I Am," "The Kind of Person I Would Like to Be," "Reading Materials that Have Changed My Attitudes, Concepts, or Behavior."

Words that I associate with myself now.

Unfinished stories.

Reactions to pictures.

Sociograms.

Interviews.

Puppetry.

Role playing.

Self-exploratory inventories.

From these attempts, it appeared that the concerns of the children fell into two categories: 1) personal concerns (especially those pertaining to the growing process, an inadequate self-concept, and loneliness) and 2) environmental concerns (peer acceptance, divorce, and relations with family members). Of course, the two categories overlap. A primary factor, such as relation with family members, may influence a secondary factor, such as peer acceptance or loneliness. The recurring themes were: overcrowded homes, absent parents, inability to learn as others do, and feeling left out and alone. Some literature, selected by reading tutors and which dramatizes these concerns, is presented in the following section.

Selecting Reading Material in Accordance with Student Needs and Concerns

Instead of approaching principle through abstract declarations, literature furnishes concrete situations exemplifying recurrent problems and themes. Character, plot, and setting furnish the background for reflective thinking about motives and values.

The reading tutors consulted reading lists furnished by the

American Council on Education and the American Library Association, as well as other lists and articles **(4).** A few selected concerns and applicable materials are listed.

CONCERNS	READING MATERIALS
1. Personal	
a. The Growing Process	a. "I Feel This Way," poem by John Ciardi; **The Growing Story** by Ruth Krauss; **Look at Me Now** by Jane Werner Watson; **A Place for Peter** by Elizabeth Yates.
b. Inadequate Self-Concept	b. **What's Wrong with Julio?** by Virginia Ormsby; **Mario, A Mexican Boy's Adventure** by Marion Garthwaite; **Juanita** by Leo Politi; **Brown Is a Beautiful Color** by Jean Carey Bond; **Who Am I?** by June Behrens; **What Is Black?** by Bettye Baker; **Black Is** by Barney Grossman.
c. Loneliness	c. **A Friend is Someone Who Likes You** by Joan Walsh Anglund; **Just Me** by Mary H. Ets; **Will I Have a Friend?** by Miriam Cohen; **Peter's Long Walk** by Lee Kingman; **Queenie Peavy** by Robert Burch; "Bereft," poem by Robert Frost.
2. Environmental	
a. Peer Acceptance	a. **Window for Rosemary** by Marguerite Vance; **Crow Boy** by Taro Yashima; **The Hundred Dresses** by Eleanor Estes; **The Empty Schoolhouse** by Natalie Savage Carlson; "You've Got a Friend" and "Alone Again, Naturally" (songs) by James Taylor.
b. Divorce	b. **It's Not the End of the World** by Judy Blume; **I'll Get There, It Better Be Worth the Trip** by John Donovan.
c. Relations with Family Members	c. **Frances** by Russell Hoban; **The Quarreling Book** by Charlotte Zolotow; **I'll Fix Anthony** by Judith Viorst; "Mama Told Me Not to Come" (song) by Three Dog Night.

It is evident that some of the reading materials may be classified under more than one concern.

Discussion techniques described in the next section were suggested to facilitate critical thinking about values.

Integrating the Process of Reading and Valuing through the Discussion of Literature

The questions included in this section are classified according to criteria derived from two sources:

a. The following are criteria underlying the process of valuing given by Raths, Harmin, and Simon **(3)**

  Choosing (1) freely
            (2) from alternatives
            (3) after thoughtful consideration of the consequences of each alternative
  Prizing   (4) cherishing, being happy with the choice
            (5) willing to affirm the choice publicly
  Acting   (6) doing something with the choice
            (7) repeatedly, in some pattern of life

b. The following criteria are from a study of significant influences of reading on concepts, attitudes, and behavior **(5)**

(1) Evidence of a combination of concept, attitude, and behavior influence
(2) Statements disclosing the development of
    (a) self-understanding
    (b) understanding of self in relation to others
    (c) understanding and empathy for others
(3) Statements showing decisions formulated
(4) Statements revealing self-observed action taken by the subject regarding decisions formulated

The teacher or discussion leader selects a dramatic moment—a major part or theme of a story, article, poem, or play—as the focus for reflective thinking and tentative decision making. The leader or discussion guide makes no moral judgments since these opinions could freeze or negate further critical and creative thinking. All ideas are discussed openly and freely as the leader elicits as many viewpoints as possible. Tentative decisions are made by the students, not the discussion leader.

Questions pertaining to the novel, **The Empty Schoolhouse** by Natalie Savage Carlson (listed under the concern of peer acceptance) are given below to illustrate the process of integrating reading and valuing. (Of course, literal questions may be asked at the beginning to clarify the understanding of the story.)

A dramatic moment in the story:

THE FIRST DAY IN AN INTEGRATED SCHOOL

Kind of Question	Purpose	Questions Stated
1. Empathy	1. Identification with a character or a situation promotes sensitivity to others. Although the affective response is predominant, some cognitive and motor reactions may be inclusive. There are degrees of empathy, of course.	1. How did Lullah feel when the big boys made fun of her as she walked to the front door of the school? How did the boys feel? How did Lullah feel when Mr. Buzzard blocked her path? How did Mr. Buzzard feel when he stepped in front of Lullah?
2. Insight	2. Empathy is related to insight (standing off and looking at ourselves from another's point of view). Emotions, however, may distort objective thinking. Here the value is explored. The reader may see himself in the situation presented or as a character in the story and perceive his place on his absorbed scale of values. Through group discussion, dimensions of values are explored giving discussants opportunities to clarify motives.	2. How would you have felt on the first day going to a new school? What would you have done if Mr. Buzzard had blocked your way to the entrance.
3. Critical Thinking	3. Weighing the consequences of alternative courses of action; testing hypotheses; relying on reason and evidence.	3. Why did Father Austin believe it was necessary to prescribe rules for the first day of school? What other rules could Father have mentioned? Why did Lullah and Emma look around for Oralee? Why did Emma let Lullah enter the school by herself? Why did Lullah keep on walking to the school when Mr. Buzzard attempted to block her

		path? Who displayed more courage, in your opinion, Lullah or Mr. Buzzard? Why? Why did Mr. Buzzard and the big boys slink away when Father Austin appeared?
4. Tentative Decision Making	4. Integrate thinking toward a tentative goal or decision on the basis of current facts and thoughtful considera- tion of the consequences of the courses of action.	4. Was Lullah's decision to enter the integrated school a wise one? Give reasons for your answer.

It is apparent from these questions that the role of the discussion leader is an important component of the reading-valuing process. This role will be explored in the next section.

Finding Out Where the Teacher Is— Needs, Values, Philosophy of Education

It has been said that there is no valueless teaching. Teacher attitude, manner, and organization for instruction reflect inherent value-structures of the individual teacher. It is suggested that the following attributes of a discussion leader or guide may contribute to the clarification of varied value patterns:

- Recognition of the worthiness of each individual.
- Respect for each participant's right to express his viewpoint.
- Positive expectancy toward the thoughts, decisions, and actions of individuals and groups to further the good in life.
- Awareness that values at home may be different from those stressed at school.
- Realization that conformity to subculture peer values may be more influential than response to adult mores.
- Realization that high assessment on the skill and competency level may not necessarily correspond to humanness.
- Acceptance of varying and conflicting points of view without alarm or judgment.
- Courage to pursue controversial issues in reflective discussion.
- Encouragement of the critical analysis of short and long term consequences of decisions and actions.
- Trust in the group realization of tentative solutions to problems.

- Commitment to listening as a teaching-learning (clarification) process.
- Willingness to learn about motives and expand awareness of peer values.
- Encouragement of autonomous responsibility for tentative decisions formulated.

Conclusion

Literature offers concrete and particular moments for the discussion of value patterns. Questions emphasizing empathy, insight, critical thinking, and tentative decision making may stimulate autonomous growth leading to integration of personality.

One of the important challenges of education, according to the late James E. Allen, Jr., former United States Commissioner of Education, is to foster attitudes, ethical standards, and behavioral patterns which will lead to our overcoming the environmental crisis in the next decades (1). Survival, amid the prevailing racial, economic, and ecological crises, demands the rejection of expedient stopgaps which may only delay further trauma. Rather, long range survival requires critical analyses of long range consequences, public affirmation of important decisions, and the courage to translate our values into humane action programs that will ensure the well being of future generations.

References

1. Allen, James E, Jr. "Statement on Environmental Education," **Nation's Schools,** 85 (April 1970), 57.
2. Keniston, Kenneth. "Youth and Violence," in Nancy F. and Theodore R. Sizer (Eds.), **Moral Education**. Cambridge, Massachusetts: Harvard University Press, 1973, 126.
3. Raths, Louis E., Merrill Harmin, and Sidney B. Simon. **Values and Teaching**. Columbus, Ohio: Charles E. Merrill, 1966, 30.
4. Riggs, Corinne W. **Bibliotherapy**. Newark, Delaware: International Reading Association, 1971.
5. Shirley, Fehl. "Case Studies of the Influence of Reading on Adolescents," **Research in the Teaching of English**, 3 (Spring 1969), 31.

ADDITIONAL SOURCES: MATERIALS

Jones, L. "Games, Games, Games—and Reading Class." **Journal of Reading,**
October 1971, 41-46.
This short article is packed with information on the purposes, sources, and
uses of games for reading instruction. It is especially valuable for teachers
of middle school and secondary students (grades 4-10). Commercial and
teacher-made games are described for such skill areas as word
recognition and analysis, vocabulary development, and comprehension
of newspapers and magazines. Also includes resource books for teachers,
as well as names and addresses of games manufacturers.

"New Materials on the Market," **Journal of Reading** and **The Reading Teacher,**
International Reading Association, published eight times yearly.
A regular feature of these two journals, appearing each year in the
January or February issues of both, this is an extensive listing of in-
structional materials newly available from commercial publishers. Each
product is described as to Type of Material, Reading Difficulty Level,
Interest Level, and Skills Developed.

Publisher's Displays at local, state, and regional reading conferences, as well as
the IRA national convention, are an excellent place to keep up to date on
recently published instructional materials.

Schubert, D. G., and T. C. Torgerson. **Improving the Reading Program** (third
edition). Dubuque, Iowa: William C. Brown Publishing, 1972.
The authors have devoted three chapters of this book to instructional
materials. Chapter 8 lists materials for correcting word recognition and
word analysis skills; Chapter 9 lists materials for improving
comprehension and study skills; Chapter 10 describes multilevel
commercial and teacher-made materials for individualizing reading
instruction.

Spache, G. D., and E. B. Spache. **Reading in the Elementary School** (fourth
edition). Boston: Allyn and Bacon, 1976.
Nearly every chapter of this popular professional text includes a listing of
commercially available instructional materials, often grouped as Skill
Development Kits, Games, Programed Materials, and Audiovisual
Materials.

Wurman, R. S. (Ed.). **Yellow Pages of Learning Resources.** Aspen, Colorado:
Invisible City International Design Conference, 1972.
This resource book should be of particular value for teachers in cities,
and especially for those who are partial to the language experience
approach. The yellow pages contain brief explanations and/or guides to
over seventy city occupations or sites from Accountant to Zoo. Also included are suggestions on using the book, and a listing of school and
community projects devoted to the neighborhood and city as learning
resources.

MATERIALS
EVALUATION
MANAGEMENT
INSTRUCTIONAL PURPOSE

Methods

In any diagnostic/prescriptive model of reading instruction, instructional materials and methods are both clearly prescriptive since they serve as vehicles for explaining, exploring, and gaining facility with important skills students need in order to become efficient readers.

Some instructional methods are built-in components of certain materials. For example, the use of a particular game, whether for teaching or for testing, implies a certain general methodology as well as the rules specific to the game itself. Other techniques, such as the cloze for comprehension training, can be applied to virtually any material. Still other instructional methods in reading demand no printed material at all, at least at first. The articles in this section represent the latter two categories.

Four instructional strategies are described. They should add to any teacher's repertoire of teaching skills. The important thing to remember with instructional methods, as with instructional materials, is that the activity or strategy must provide a clear opportunity for necessary student involvement in one or more important facets of the reading process. These methods are only representative; the teacher with a clear understanding of fluent reading behavior (see Section One) can easily generate additional methods which contribute to reading growth when prescribed according to identified student needs.

The Natural Cluster Method

ABRAHAM GREENFIELD
Kingsborough Community College

In 1960, Dolch (1) reported that "children enter first grade knowing 2,000 to 3,000 word meanings." Estimates today are higher. Yet, first graders are required to learn to read only 250 to 300 words. Poor readers learn less than half this number.

A large number of commonly used meaningful words can be elicited in a few minutes from a group of children through the use of a word-association game that is fun and challenging. This activity results in success responses and helps counteract the tendency so prevalent among reading retardates to develop a sense of failure.

The Technique

A game is begun by saying, "I'm thinking of the word _____ (e.g., water); what does the word **water** make you think of?" Responses from kindergarten and older children include **drink, wash, swim, ocean, rain.** This is an example of a natural word cluster. The word **water** is called the **starter word.**

Each response is greeted by the teacher with a rewarding "good," "right," or "yes," and is written on the board forming a list under the starter word. This list is copied by students. Response words (and occasional phrases) are, of course, meaningful to the child and at times spring directly from his culture.

Next, children are asked to create sentences using the words listed. Frequent responses to the water cluster are, "I drink water." "I like to swim in the ocean." Within a few minutes, perhaps a dozen words are on the board and copied into notebooks. Students are then asked to volunteer a word to start the next game.

Here we have the middle-class teacher in an innercity school making the core of her reading lesson out of words and expressions natural to the neighborhoods and backgrounds of her students. At the same time, the teacher is learning the language as well as the patterns of activities of the local culture. Further, the children learn from one another. In integrated or multiethnic classes, there is also cross-cultural learning and acceptance of one another's language, because the teacher has expressed approval of every response.

Starter-words are presented either by students or teacher and can originate from objects and activities familiar in school, home, street, or other area. Sources of teacher starter-words include difficult words from interesting stories, from Experience Charts, from Show and Tell, and even from basal readers. Any kind of art work or picture is an excellent starting stimulus. The teacher should feel free to give her own associations in words familiar to the children. End of session review of words and sentences can include questions on phonics and spelling.

Recognition and Comprehension

Weeks later, children recognize these word clusters and sentences (many of which are beyond the Dolch list) because

1. The guaranteed success in terms of teacher acceptance of every associative response produces mounting enthusiasm and interest, and virtually 100 percent attention. (Here is the cognitive emphasis on attention and motivation produced by reinforcement.)

2. An experiment by Parker and Noble (2) showed that learning could be improved by artificially increasing the number of associations to a verbal stimulus. This experiment supports the contention that a large number of readily available associations to a starter-word aids in its recognition. (In the previous example, the word **water** should be more easily recognized after its association cluster has been developed by the children.) Further, comprehension of more difficult starter-words is enhanced because the cluster network of associations enriches the connotative structure supporting the starter-word.

3. Rouse and Verinis (3) showed that recognition of one word improves the chances of subsequent recognition of any of its associates; for example, recognition of the word **water** facilitates recognition of **drink, swim,** and **ocean.**

Applications

The natural cluster method can be applied in a variety of ways, limited only by the teacher's ingenuity and imagination. If a story is to be read by the teacher or the children, key words or phrases can be "gamed" before the story is read, and the difficult words after it is read. The next time the story is read, recognition errors are fewer, and comprehension is likely to be more thorough. Hence, interesting stories and even school-magazine or newspaper clippings can be used, in spite of the fact that they contain words beyond the grade level. As mentioned earlier, Experience Charts and Show and Tell activities provide an excellent source of more advanced starter-stimuli. An interview with the custodian or with a member of a local community establishment will not be restricted to first grade words.

As soon as children become aware that drawings, pictures, or toys are used to start the game, many such items are submitted to the teacher. The most productive pictures are those of animals, children, and families. An appropriate question is, "What does this picture make you think of?" It is not necessary to interrupt the trend of spontaneous reaction to the picture by writing while the children are talking. Key words and phrases can be written after several responses have occurred.

Word Confusion

A common problem among poor readers is one of confusing words that are similar in appearance (for example, **three/there, parent/pocket**). Using each as a starter-word, and comparing the wide differences in association, strengthens differentiation.

Individual Differences

Experience in pilot studies has shown that hyperactive children volunteer most often and give the most varied associations. They also score highest in reviews and tests.

The withdrawn, dull child looks startled each time his answer is labeled "right" or "good." During the first games, such a child may not volunteer until a leading question is directed to him; for example, to the starter-word **water,** the question could be, "What does the word **water** make a sailor (or a mother) think of?"

Personality Development

In general, it has been found that a sense of achievement, a sense of competence, eventually develops to replace that sense of failure so evident among reading retardates. Creativity begins to appear as the children learn to risk their thoughts, fantasies, hypotheses—as it dawns upon them that someone is interested in listening to them. Later in the year, a story can be written around the associations to a word or picture.

The Game at Home

Children have been able to play the game at home with parents, siblings, or friends. The class or group can choose a word or two to use as starters outside of school. Many children show obvious pride the next day in telling the words these starters elicited. Parent workshops, or even a letter to parents, can show how the game can be played around the dinner table.

No writing is required in this "homework." Hence, the game often proceeds in chain fashion: word A elicits word B which then becomes the stimulus-word to elicit word C, and so on. With a word like **water,** results at home do not differ much from the classroom game; but the word **look** could yield **eyes** which could itself evoke **nose,** an unlikely response to **look.** This chain variation of the game is used in kindergarten classes where it promotes reading readiness by enlarging verbal experience. Thus, even five-year-olds begin to learn words from each other, from each other's cultures, and from the teacher's associations.

Difficult Words

Abstract words, which are less meaningful to children, are more difficult but usually evoke concrete associations. For example, to the abstract word **property,** one child's response was, "Keep off, private property"; to **information,** responses included **telephone** and **library.**

The least meaningful of words, the small and familiar-to-children prepositions and conjunctions (e.g., **of, or,** and **and**) are the bane of the poor reader. Actually, these words are concepts that perform functions in phrases and sentences.

These **function words** are taught most effectively by embedding them in a large number of meaningful concrete phrases. For example:

bread and _____   candy or cake

Jack and _____   play ball or_____

_____and _____   _____or_____

The children volunteer familiar combinations themselves, such as spaghetti and meatballs, ball and bat, etc. Leads are supplied by the teacher only if necessary.

The function words can be in a continuing unit on "connecting words," a phrase which children understand. With brighter children, it is possible to elicit the actual concept that some of the connecting words represent. Asking "Can you think of a word that covers this whole list?" yields **partners** and **together** for the "and" list; **deciding** and **choosing** for the "or" list. Each concept acts as an umbrella for a list of concrete phrases. The longer the list or cluster of phrases, the stronger the base for understanding and retaining the concept and its function.

Results

Pilot work with the natural cluster method was highly successful with first and second grade classes, with small groups of reading retardates in corrective reading, and with classes of older retarded children. Integrated and multiethnic groups naturally provided a greater variety of responses and of intercultural learning. Given to kindergarten classes for reading readiness, participation was excellent and enjoyment obvious.

A group of five second grade reading retardates seen for one forty minute period per week read fluently over 90 percent of the words and sentences they had created more than a month earlier. The principal of the school said, "This technique motivates the unmotivated."

A conservative estimate of words learned should be an average of ten new words per forty minute lesson per day. (Later in the year, words learned previously will show up. However, this will be compensated for by the greater facility the children develop, resulting in a greater number of associations.)

In 3 sessions per week, or about 100 sessions per year, this gives a total of about 1,000 words created by children from their own vocabularies. If only half the words are retained by year's end, 500 familiar words will have been learned.

Conclusion

A great advantage of the natural cluster technique is that it can be used as a basic program, as a supplement to any ongoing program, or for a small group corrective or remedial reading program. Once the teachers have mastered the technique, using it costs nothing.

References

1. Dolch, E. W. **Teaching Primary Reading**. Champaign, Illinois: Garrard, 1960.
2. Parker, C. V., and C. E. Noble. "Experimentally Produced Meaningfulness in Paired-Associate Learning," **American Journal of Psychology**, 76 (1963), 579-588.
3. Rouse, R. O., and J. S. Verinis. "The Effect of Asssociative Connections on the Recognition of Flashed Cards," **Journal of Verbal Learning and Verbal Behavior**, 1 (1963), 300-303.

Action Oriented Strategies

CARL L. ROSEN
Kent State University

There are many pupils whose reading is characterized by non-fluent and inaccurate oral reading, or ineffective and inefficient silent reading comprehension. Such pupils read slowly, hesitating frequently to study unfamiliar words. They are often unsuccessful in their efforts to identify problem words, and their errors consistently reveal imbalanced decoding strategies, that is, close graphophonemic approximation, but little attention to semantic and grammatic information available through context. In other words, many pupils inadequately "self-monitor" when processing print and their rate and accuracy of literal comprehension in silent reading is seriously impaired. Such pupils are reluctant to begin and maintain reading behavior and break away as soon as they are able. Lengthy passages are very difficult for them and reading is not perceived as a meaningful experience. Their responses to reading are sources of teacher concern and, sometimes, parental hysteria. Clinical work with such pupils often reveals a history of inflexible instructional overemphasis in the use of phonics in learning to read.

We have been designing alternative instructional experiences for such children through applications of information from the literature in reading and psycholinguistics. Our aim has been to develop and explore the use of functional reading experiences that are of high motivational value. These strategies are designed to develop automatic comprehension responses to print, to tap the cognitive and linguistic resources of pupils, and to foster pupil independence in monitoring their own reading. We have found that, when intelligently managed and creatively implemented, systematic exposure to such experiences is not only helpful for problem readers but equally facilitative in fostering reading growth for other pupils. The Action Oriented Reading Strategy (AO) described in this paper is one of these approaches.

The Action Oriented Reading Strategy

The basic goal of AO is to foster rapid, automatic comprehension responses to print. This involves systematically exposing pupils to printed directions that are easily read, rapidly and silently comprehended, and constructed so that they result in observable pupil actions and activities, hence the term, "Action Oriented."

The success of the AO strategy depends on message construction. With creativity and care in message construction, print becomes a live medium. Simple messages are constructed that involve finding hidden objects, doing favorite chores, going to work with a friend, or consulting with the teacher. Well constructed messages should involve acts that provide immediate feedback to the pupils so they know their reading was successful. For example, if pupils are given a message that there is something for them under a table, the "surprise" they find should be labeled with their names. Pupils must understand that the approach involves reading the message and following the message directions immediately. (At first, many separate the reading from the relevant actions that should ensue.)

Length and readability of messages should be carefully controlled and systematically increased as responses become more rapid. Messages at first should be in short, simple, active sentences, imbedded with vocabulary from reading series, or highly redundant words from useful word lists, such as the one developed by Harris and Jacobson (1). Simple one-stage messages, consisting of single sentences, can be enlarged into two and three stage directions. Eventually, multiple-sequence messages can be placed at several different locations, and the highly enjoyable "Treasure Hunt" tactic (described below) can be experienced.

To enhance motivation, independent problem solving, and social interaction among pupils, messages should answer the questions What? Who? and Where? Several pupils can work in teams to read and follow the same message. Teams can be given similar but slightly different messages. Conversation and interaction in dealing with messages should be encouraged, and explanations on how to solve message problems should be given. Identical messages can be repeated to provide frequent and systematic exposure to reading vocabulary still being learned. Messages can be transformed by varying words, modifying sentences, or substituting words that alter directions subtly or significantly. Creative teachers can cause surprise effects for the benefit and enjoyment of students.

The teacher, of course, remains aware of the pupils' abilities to deal with this function of print as well as their personal satisfaction. Regular discussions by teacher and pupils, both before and after AO experiences, help students to read messages rapidly, make sure their understanding of what they must do "makes sense and sounds right," and act immediately in appropriate ways. Teachers should illustrate the kinds of word identification problems unfamiliar words present, and how to deal flexibly with distinctive features in the framework of context. Pupils should explain to others how they dealt with such problems, how they knew when they were right, when they knew they must try again, and when a single word did or did not interfere with message comprehension.

To extend and advance AO beyond teacher constructed messages, ideal stimulus inputs for pupils are their own Language Experience production of directions, which they dictate, copy, or write themselves. Writing directions (in manuscript) for others to follow must be carefully handled, but this enlivens the experience, maintains momentum, and exposes pupils to more interesting tasks. After much success with straight prose experiences (AOsp) we have been reducing simple directions into what we call "novel tasks" (AOnt). This involves deleting selected words to encourage use of contextual information, risk taking, and forward scanning of sentences. Other AOnt approaches can involve giving directions in Jumbled Word Order, Scrambled Phrases, Mutilated Orthography, Pseudo Words, Irrelevantly Imbedded Words, and Code. Much care is recommended in construction of AOnt messages, as illustrated in this paper and discussed elsewhere **(5).**

Some Illustrations

The following AO tactics serve only to illustrate the possibilities available to teachers for enhancing reading through supplemental use of this approach.

Simon Says Reading Game should be an outgrowth of the traditional listening game, via rapid visual exposure and responses to the very same commands as listening. The printed AO message equivalents are placed on game cards. A collection of cards is built by the teacher from her own tape recorded oral commands of Simon Says games. Initially, the cards might be used parallel with the tape recorded spoken commands. With practice, the pupils should soon respond to the printed cards alone. When children collect enough command words they can construct their own cards and the game can change to "Billy Says" or "Alice Says." The complexity of printed commands is increased over the year. The listening aspect of the game can be regularly interspersed with the reading. Systematic practice and increasingly more rapid responses to repeated messages contribute to automatic comprehension responses. The teacher is particularly sensitive to less successful readers and pupils who become easily embarrassed in public.

Teacher Says Game involves development of a basic set of cards containing short, simple directions for classroom routines which are usually given orally by the teacher. Initially, spoken and printed directions might be alternated to better connect the two functions and obtain optimum attention to the visual features of directions. The frequency and complexity of these printed AO experiences are systematically increased by the teacher and differentially practiced by the whole class, groups, or individuals. Direct instruction and word collections could be implemented for specific pupils having difficulties. Examples of directions are: "Raise your hand if you want a hot lunch." "Line up for gym." "You have ten minutes to clean your desks."

What To Do Game involves more specific directions for particular classwork via blackboard, bulletin board, flannel board, or printed materials for whole class, groups, or individuals. Pupils now respond AO fashion to a variety of printed directions involving more detailed and multistage classroom assignments such as obtaining equipment, working on the correct subjects, or turning work in to designated places. Pupils may consult with one another to deal with the directions. However, the teacher should note pupils having difficulty with messages, and plan follow-up activities that would involve work with these particular pupils. Here again, vocabulary difficulty and sentence complexity are gradually and carefully increased.

Personal Notes to pupils from their teacher, other teachers, the principal, or other children, thanking them for their assistance, complimenting good work, inviting them to come and visit, to see something special, or to join them in some activity or event are also of value in providing AOsp experiences.

Announcements for Swapping and trading objects involve thinking out and preparing simple messages on what pupils have to swap and what they might wish to obtain. This involves either teacher recorded (language experience dictated) and pupil copied swap cards, or pupil preparation of their own cards. The trick here is not to identify the writer by name, but to describe what he/she will be wearing on Swap Day (colors, clothes, appearance) and what he/she will have to trade. Everyone must read the cards in class (or between classes) to know who they are dealing with. Plan carefully; it can get wild! AOsp only is advised.

Detailed Directions can be provided in print for pupils of higher reading ability. Appropriate materials are supplied and through printed messages, pupils are directed to assemble equipment, build models, complete bulletin boards for the teacher, follow recipes, perform science experiments, learn rules for new games, or practice steps in square dancing. This tactic, as with the others, places the emphasis in reading on immediate comprehension.

The Treasure Hunt is probably the most enjoyable tactic of the AO strategy. As soon as minimal reading ability develops, hunts can be initiated. This tactic provides direct immediate feedback for comprehension responses; that is, as messages are comprehended new messages are quickly located and the treasure is finally found. It may involve two, three, or even more multistage messages when these are appropriate. Multistage AO messages involve a whole series of message parts, each being dependent upon comprehending prior stages. Easily accomplished treasure hunts are provided at first, with carefully controlled readability. Pupils enjoy the mystique of treasure hunting, joining their friends in the search for a treasure in mysterious places in the classroom, school building, or on the playground. School principals, nurses, custodians, and other personnel enjoy being involved. Physical activity and social interaction turn reading into a satisfying experience. The messages move from short and easy to tasks of gradually increasing complexity. Sometimes, envelopes with pupils' names printed on the front and placed in unexpected places can turn a classroom or reading center into a place that children cannot wait to enter. What To Do Games can be easily developed into Treasure Hunts. The age level for utilizing this tactic can span the elementary and middle school years.

After much mastery with straight prose hunts, other messages can be reduced into AOnt. Samples include **Semantic Distortion:** "Find the red UFO on the teacher's Planet. Turn to YEAR 26 for the next note." **Semantic Cueing:** "Go to the (place where we keep our chalk). Under the (thing that we keep the yellow chalk in) you will find the treasure." **Mutilated Orthography:** "Look under the third seat in row one." **Irrelevant Imbedded Items** (Cryptography): "Your purple treasure red is green under brown the orange book pink next yellow to blue the violet fishtank." **Cloze Deletions:** "The last person _____ the last row _____ our room is _____ on an envelope _____ your name on _____." **Vowel Deletions:** "You w_ll find y_ _r note n_ _r the pl_c_ you dr_nk water _n our r_ _m."

AOnt directions such as the following may also be tried. **Jumbled Word Order:** "spelling Finish assignment your page 15 on." **Scrambled Phrases**: "your own questions/Make up/on this week's/news events/for others/to answer." Stringing Word Order: "Weneedanameforourclass-petthattellsaboutwhathedidtoday. Leaveyoursuggestionwithyourclass-secretary." **Coded Messages**: ☑ ☒ ☉ ◙ ☉ is a note ☑ ☉ your desk for ◙ ☉ ☻. (Note: Pupils must have the code with alphabetic equivalents. The note above is "There is a note in your desk for you.") The Coding

Approach is more fully described elsewhere **(6)**.

As students increase their abilities to deal efficiently with simple forms of AO, more socially relevant and mature AO experiences should be provided. "Want Ads" have been initiated by teachers on a class, interclass, or schoolwide basis. Pupil prepared AO index cards may be posted and read before "Swap Days." Pupils may write directions for solving math word problems, questions in the content areas, puzzles, construction activities, or ideas for "getting along" with teachers and parents.

Summary

AO is a promising alternative reading strategy which offers directive types of functional reading experiences for pupils. It emphasizes rapid information processing and, when creatively designed, captivates the attention of pupils by making reading acts relevant and enjoyable experiences. It is particularly useful for "word bound" and immature readers. Systematic, regular exposure creates a building-up of proficiency in reading comprehension and its underlying skills and abilities. Pupils gradually shift attention to extracting meanings rather than studying words.

The approach can be used with most pupils. The unique demands for attention to meaning and the highly motivating conditions associated with activity, action, and immediate feedback of results contribute to the potential impact on improving both attitudes and competency in reading.

The strategy must, however, be intelligently, sensitively, and thoughtfully applied for pupils to develop automatic comprehension responses. It is important to understand that pupils' actions after reading well constructed messages are readily observable, whereas required oral reading to ascertain precise word identification is often counterproductive.

Although the approach is only experimental, a whole range of tactics could be designed by those who understand AO principles, who sense the possibilities inherent in their use, and who are willing and able to take time to carefully design appropriate experiences. These must be carefully evaluated, refined, and systematically included in daily work. AO is an alternative strategy for providing a type of functional reading experience, not a systematic self-contained program. The approach represents a kind of reading experience pupils need if they are to achieve maximum growth in reading.

References

1. Harris, A., and M. Jacobson. **Basic Elementary Reading Vocabularies**. New York: Macmillan, 1972.
2. Kaluger, G., and C. Kolson. **Reading and Learning Disabilities**. Columbus, Ohio: Charles E. Merrill, 1969, 243-244.
3. McDade, James. "Beginning Reading By a Non-Oral Method," **Seventh Yearbook of the National Elementary Principal**, 17 (March 1937), 305-312.
4. McDade, J. **Essentials of Non-Oral Beginning Reading**. Chicago: Plymouth, 1941.
5. Rosen, C. "Reading and the Disadvantaged: Some Psycholinguistic Applications for the Classroom Teacher," in T. Barrett and D. Johnson (Eds.), **Views on Elementary Reading Instruction**. Newark, Delaware: International Reading Association, 1973, 12-21.
6. Rosen, C., and S. Tibbals. "Coding: An Instructional Technique for Teaching Reading to Severely Disabled and Immature Readers," in J. Johns (Ed.), **Literacy for Diverse Learners**. Newark, Delaware: International Reading Association, 1974, 71-77.
7. Thompson, H. **An Experimental Study of the Beginning Reading of Deaf Mutes**. Contributions to Education, No. 254, New York Teacher's College, Columbia University, 1927.

Affective Strategies at the Secondary Level

ANN P. WILLIAMSON
North Texas State University

Educators, as well as mental health professionals, are becoming increasingly aware of the important role of public schools in providing a suitable setting for the development of positive self-concept and self-esteem among students. This awareness is based on three premises: 1) the school is the one institution which reaches all children and adolescents, 2) the student years appear to be the best time for intervention, and 3) the teacher is the best agent through whom to operate such a program (6:481).

During the sixties, many educators began to view teachers as technologists who distributed programed instruction booklets, kept the computer consoles in working order, and tuned in to the correct educational television channel. By the beginning of the seventies, however, the role of the teacher was being redefined as that of facilitator of student affective and cognitive development, rather than merely a transmitter of knowledge.

Affective Teaching

The 1970 yearbook of the Association for the Supervisors of Curriculum Development (ASCD) expressed in essence that the commitment to the seventies is "to nurture humaneness" or to develop humane individuals. As promising as they may be, innovations such as the open classroom, team teaching, competency based instruction, and improved media cannot substitute for those qualities in a teacher that make learning possible (2).

What are teacher qualities which have been indicated in the literature as being superior in the affective domain? Combs (1) listed these as traits characteristic of good teachers in the affective areas:

1. Helping rather than dominating
2. Understanding rather than condemning
3. Accepting rather than rejecting
4. Valuing integrity rather than violating integrity
5. Being positive rather than negative

6. Being open rather than closed to experience
7. Being tolerant of ambiguity rather than intolerant.

Taba and Elkins (**7**: 265) described the kind of teachers needed: "Students need to see that the teacher cares, that she is a human being who is interested in them personally...finds ways to make a student feel good about himself...and helps students through some crises."

Teachers who view themselves as a part of a therapeutic process act differently from those who see themselves strictly as content specialists. Of all the school forces, the teacher undoubtedly has the strongest influence over the developing and emerging student. Beginning with Pygmalian and continuing through subsequent studies, the evidence from research is clear that teacher expectations can encourage student achievement or cause failure. Seventy percent of the school day is spent in teacher-pupil interaction. This continual interaction, both overt and subtle, is the means used to transmit clear, value laden messages (3:413).

Few students see methods and materials as decisive educational factors, and fewer adults recollect great texts, but nearly everyone remembers some great teacher.

It would appear that most teacher training institutions are doing an adequate job of teaching secondary teachers cognitive strategies in their specialized areas. Fewer institutions are dealing with affective strategies. Affective strategies are those which attempt to make the student understand himself, feel better about himself and, in turn, respond positively to the curriculum. Affective teaching is particularly important at the secondary level when the student is facing the problems of adolescence—physical change, sex, social development, identity, values, and alienation.

Literature

One of the most commonly accepted affective strategies at the secondary level is that of improving self-concept through the use of literature, commonly referred to as bibliotherapy.

The teacher must be aware of the problems existing in his particular classroom and provide books which will enable him to help his students work through their problems. Students in a racially torn community may profit from the group reading and discussion of the popular novel **Brian's Song,** available in paperback form. This novel deals with the intimate friendship of two athletes—one black, one white. Discussion might include questions such as, What joys were encountered in this friendship? What risks were encountered? What risks were due to the fact that the two were of different races? What risks are involved in any friendship, whether racially mixed or not? What hardships did the main characters face then that would not be a problem in today's society?

Emotional development can be enhanced through the reading and discussion of books. Some suggestions are provided by Landau, et al. (3).

Subject	Suggested Book	Author
Love	Don't You Wish You Were Dead	L. Woiwode
Jealousy	All Summer in a Day	Ray Bradbury
Fear	The Dog	Carol Reilley
Courage	A Day's Wait	E. Hemingway
Compassion	Winter Night	Kay Boyle
Anger	The White Circle	John Clayton
Shame	A Tree Grows in Brooklyn	Betty Smith
Concept of Self	The Web and the Rock	Thomas Wolfe

One teacher has reported a highly successful game used in connection with affective strategies through literature. She has described "Roadblocks" which was played by the class following a student-directed discussion of **Go Tell It On the Mountain** by James Baldwin. Students were asked to name obstacles which hindered the main character in his quest for self-fulfillment. They labeled positions on the floor of the classroom and marked them as roadblocks with chairs and other objects. As students encountered in their reading such roadblocks as parental pressure, white racism, or guilt, they labeled them and discussed them in relationship to their own lives. Based on this experience, students were asked to draw roadblocks of their own lives, listing barriers to their own achievements.

Students may express their innermost thoughts through the reading of a particular book, assuming the role of the protagonist, and writing a diary entry. Extremely poignant diary entries have been written after students have read and discussed "The Blue Parakeets" by H.C. Branner from **Two Minutes of Silence.** Katrine is an emotionally disturbed child who is seriously handicapped in her ability to relate to other children and adults. Demands, which she cannot possibly fulfill, are placed upon her by her family and by school personnel. Her parakeets are her one joy in life, and she eventually gives them away. Even seemingly nonverbal students are able to become quite articulate when asked to write, as in a diary entry, how Katrine felt the day she gave away her parakeets.

Music

Music is an important aspect of the modern youth culture. A listing of affective strategies would have to include use of music in the classroom. One of the most popular uses of music in the classroom is examination of lyrics of modern songs. Many of the lyrics are intriguing enough to cause serious thought and discussion of what the song writer is trying to communicate. For predominately black groups, or groups particularly interested in black culture, lyrics of songs such as James Brown's "I'm Black and I'm Proud" and Nina Simone's, "To Be Young, Gifted, and Black" are useful. Many of John Denver's lyrics deal seriously with ecology and the beauty of nature, subjects which could be useful discussion starters. Other lyrics enjoyed by youth are satires on current political situations. Many secondary students would be pleased to bring the lyrics of their favorite songs to school and discuss their meanings with the class.

Many youth who are deficient in verbal skills, may be talented instrumental players. They can be challenged to write original lyrics and set them to music to be played and sung for the class. This could be in lieu of book reports which "turn off" many students.

Language Experience

Language experience, usually associated with the elementary grades, is certainly a viable method of improving reading skills of secondary students. The idea, of course, is that what a student can think, he can say; what he can say, can be written; what can be written, can be read. In this day of energy shortages we may not be able to take students on long field trips to provide them with common experiences, but there are things and places in their own cities or neighborhoods which they may have missed.

Plan an awareness walk and ask each student to find an object, examine it carefully, and be prepared to write a descriptive account of it when he returns to the classroom. Many students may enjoy something as simple as a walk through the parking lot to discover a car to serve as the basis for his writing. After all, wouldn't a description of a Porsche be as valuable in improving communication skills as the proverbial "What I Did Last Summer" theme?

Writing assignments can become new and exciting experiences for youth when based on interpreting the colorful pop posters which are so readily available and which are accepted by today's youth. Bring several into the classroom and post them on the walls. Assign each student to select a poster, study its message through both the caption and the art work, and write his impression. Sharing impressions might be a good culminating activity or, if artistically and philosophically inclined, their own pop posters might be made for display.

Drama

Drama and skits are effective strategies for improving self-concept at the secondary level. Some more daring teachers may want to begin at the beginning and acutally have the class write a play, cast it, and build the sets to produce it for other classes. A project of this nature is described by Saraceno and Piscitello (5). Other, less adventurous teachers may want to select a play or skit already written and have the class act it out. Students gain several benefits from drama: cooperating with class members, overcoming inhibitions as they play certain roles, and learning to accept risks of performing before their peers. Through drama, students often discover skills of which they were unaware.

Case Study and Role Play

Openness in class discussion is achieved when students know that their contribution will at least be listened to and respected, if not agreed with. There are several effective methods of achieving good class discussion. One particularly effective method is that of using case studies, especially when dealing in the realm of personal development. Begin by writing a real situation about a young person, or one which suggests realism in its problem and detail. Develop several questions to be used as a guide for class discussion. Often, students can discuss problems of others and come up with satisfying solutions which can, in turn, be related to their own personal problems. The value of case study is that students are objectively discussing problems of others, rather than facing the embarrassment of displaying their own personal problems.

The technique of role play is closely related to the use of case studies. A situation is read or told to the group and class members are asked to assume the identity of the person in the situation. One teacher reported reading a story of a gang initiation in a large city. In the situation, the final act of the initiation was to walk a pole suspended between two buildings at the fortieth story level. After the reading of the situation, the question was posed, "What would you have done if you had been faced with this situation?"

Projective Techniques

Several projective techniques can be used to help students begin to examine themselves and their relationships with others. For years, dating back to before the World War II slogan "Kilroy was here," youth have been expressing their innermost feelings on fences, walls, buses, and subways. This type of graffiti has been particularly revealing about the self-concept and self-esteem of the writers. Allow students to make their own graffiti board in the classroom by hanging a long sheet of butcher paper across one of the walls. Have available different colors of felt tip pens, crayons, or colored chalk. Allow students to write messages for each other and for members of other classes. Teachers who have used this technique report that students usually set their own ground rules for eliminating obscenities. If not, the teacher will have to intervene and set the limitations. Even the most disabled readers will be able to make contributions to the graffiti board and read what others have written. The messages will be sad, funny, poignant, and sometimes even nonsensical, but they will be reflective of what students feel.

Another effective projective technique is the playing of the game, "Who Am I?" Each student completes five sentences about himself, each beginning "I am...." The students guess the identity of the writer from the messages. In one class where this was done a student answered, "I am depressed, I am socially walled in, I am confused, I am struggling for identity, I am searching for strength to face reality." The students quickly guessed who had written the statements. One student explained, "I can tell by what you say in class that you are really a sensitive person. You seem to be trying to get yourself together as the paper says" (4:310).

Other projective techniques include assigning each student to tear construction paper into a shape that is representative of his own uniqueness, and to explain his representation orally to the class. When this was done recently, one student who rarely makes an oral contribution in class, tore his piece of construction paper into a track shoe, with tiny cleats protruding from the bottom. When asked to explain, he told the class about his interest in the school track program, making them aware of a side of the student which the others rarely saw. From that time on, the class members and the teacher watched the school and local newspaper for news of Clayton's track successes.

One other projective technique is the use of a graph to help students plot strengths and weaknesses. Ask each student to make a graph with numbers 1-5 vertically and 1-10 horizontally as shown.

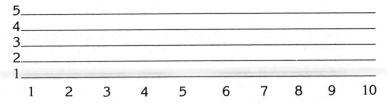

	1	2	3	4	5	6	7	8	9	10

As a class activity, ask students to let number 3 (vertical) represent most of the students in the school. Level 5 is ideal, with level 1 being least desirable. As each question (numbered horizontally) is read, have each student plot where on the graph he would fall. All information should be kept confidential.

1. Where are you in ability to make friends?
2. Where are you in mathematical ability?
3. Where are you in musical ability?
4. Where are you in personal appearance?
5. Where are you in ability to make good grades?
6. Where are you in mechanical ability?
7. Where are you in ability to have a good time?
8. Where are you in classroom behavior?
9. Where are you in reading ability?
10. Where are you in athletic ability?

Direct students to join all the dots as in a line graph. Instruct the students to write one sentence for a conclusion and ask them to share their conclusions with each other, if they wish. Usually, they will be somewhat alike representing the idea, "I am good in some things, poor in others." Sharing will help them to see that this is generally true with all people.

Conclusion

To teach effectively, we must teach affectively; we must teach students to like themselves. Building self-concept and self-esteem and helping students understand and accept their own strengths and limitations, should be a major focus of every secondary teacher.

References

1. Combs, Arthur. **The Professional Education of Teachers: A Perceptual View of Teacher Preparation.** Boston: Allyn and Bacon, 1965.
2. Hanna, Lavonne. "An Education Imperative: Commitment to Change," **To Nurture Humaneness: Commitment for the '70s,** 1970 Yearbook.

Washington, D.C.: Association for the Supervision of Curriculum Development, 1970.

3. Landau, Elliot, Sherrie Epstein, and Ann Stone. **Child Development through Literature**. Englewood Cliffs, New Jersey: Prentice-Hall, 1972.

4. Reggy, Mae A. "Self-Identity through Literature," **College English**, 35 (December 1973), 307-311.

5. Saraceno, Joseph A., and Angelina C. Piscitello. "A Play! A Homemade Play!" **Journal of Reading**, 17 (October 1973), 44-46.

6. Schulman, Jerome L., Robin C. Ford, and Patricia Busk. "Classroom Program to Improve Self-Concept," **Psychology and the Schools**, 10 (October 1973), 481-487.

7. Taba, Hilda, and Deborah Elkins. **Teaching Strategies for the Culturally Disadvantaged**. Chicago: Rand McNally, 1966.

Language Research by Children

JOHN P. SHEPARD
Skidmore College

Eight fifth graders individually count the words on a separate page in **Webster's Third Unabridged Dictionary,** add their figures, divide the total by eight, and multiply the average obtained by 2,256 (the number of pages found in the printed dictionary). The students learn that the dictionary contains 314,000 words.

A boy finds three words in an 1871 edition of Webster's unabridged, none of which are listed in the current edition. He is now pursuing the question, "Where do words go?"

Two boys invent a word, derive its various forms, and plot secretly to start using it around school. Their question is, "How do words come into the language?"

Several students try to rewrite a Middle English facsimile of an anecdote by William Caxton, the earliest known English printer. The whole class is divided into two groups—one to find all the sounds of English, the other to start collecting the variety of spellings.Organizational and research problems arise. Should they use a chart of spellings on the front cover of a dictionary? Many list word after word using the same spelling for a given sound, even after they are told that only one example is needed of each different spelling. The sound searchers are told to try picking the sounds out of any twenty word chunk of writing. They struggle with the teacher to find how many distinct sounds there are in "chunk." They feel their jaws, listen, try to hear /ng/ preceding the final /k/. Contrasting sequences of whole class sounding /a/ /e/ /i/ /o/ /u/ followed by /f/ /s/ /p/ /t/ with hands across the front of their throats they begin to discover "voice." From a small list on the board (**level, pep, rotor, refer**), a few students immediately offer **pop, radar, noon**. Six who need work on articulating some sounds are given a mirror to use to see, as well as feel, what happens when they pronounce certain sounds. They are asked to draw a cutaway profile of head and shoulders and to indicate parts of themselves they use in making speech sounds. They argue, "Is the tongue in the same position when saying the first sound in **thick** and **this?**" Everybody gets a partner.

Pairs are assigned twenty pages in the reader to survey for slang or dialect in any writing between quotation marks. Many students don't recall what quotation marks are; a few vaguely curved shapes, "like new moons." "No, I think they go the other way." The teacher asks, "Is it only a line?" Someone tries to compare the shape to a comma, but can't recall the name, **comma.** Someone else supplies it. They look in the reader to see exactly how quotation marks are printed and find the teacher has reversed the placement of the "ball-like" part.

That's an unrepresentative sample of what this report is about—unrepresentative because samples only begin to suggest the vast areas of linguistic material children can explore by research. Sure, most of it has been done before by recognized scholars; but children as researchers may learn more, and learn more vividly, about their language by investigating it directly. The nature of language is often hidden, rather than revealed, by the text and workbook exercises assigned. Further, most teachers recognize the minimal degree of involvement and motivation by children in continually doing such exercises.

Cautions and Implications

Research by children is not likely to be the ultimate panacea. Look at the history of new ideas and methods. Programed instruction in the early sixties led to English 2600, which used the ridiculous nineteenth century approach to grammar. Paul Roberts did a beautiful job of integrating structural and transformational grammars, but in one of the most didactic and unrewarding series of language texts. The earliest linguistic readers slipped back into the stilted and overly repetitive style of the "look-look-oh-oh-see-see" pattern. Some used picture clues, others wiped out illustration altogether. Personalized methods like Gattegno's Words in Colour, Ashton-Warner's organic reading, and Mae Carden's phonics were too closely linked to an often brilliantly creative originating teacher. Perhaps the method most like research is the language experience approach, where children use their own talk and writing or a class developed experience chart for reading. But, in a discouragingly large number of classrooms, children apathetically copy the daily chart because the teacher tells them to, just about as routine as the daily round robin oral reading of an assigned reader story. So watch out! Research, too, can be institutionalized and "curriculumerated"—doled out in spirit duplicator editions or added to text chapters as "enrichment" exercises. It is better to have long lists of possible research projects in all conceivable linguistic areas and resist scoping and sequencing.

If many teachers react negatively to workbook and drill exercises and bewail their fate in trying to keep children attentive for turns at oral reading; if children (while doing drill exercises) get so much wrong, copy blindly, forget, dawdle, and become identified as problem children or slow learners, then other types of experiences seem in order. Rejecting the extremes of coddling, fun, undue love, or absolute obedience, perhaps two key motivations need to be reexamined: children doing things that are so often done for them by adults, and children doing things because they are difficult. Researchers try to keep the Hawthorne effect minimized; it seems reasonable that teachers should deliberately try to take maximum advantage of the Hawthorne effect. New ideas do reflect a concern by the idea producer for those involved—the students—and this can work to the benefit of the learners only through increased motivation.

Implementation

Weaving research by children into the established curriculum can be accomplished by the teacher with little difficulty. Simply by using the existing language texts and curriculum, teachers can match topics such as phonics, word meaning, syntax, spelling, and language structure to specific, related research matters. Study of affixes, irregular or strong verbs, or multiple meanings of words can be revealed by comparing Latin, Greek, and Anglo-Saxon affixes; word origins with side trips into tribal movements; writings of King Alfred, Chaucer, or Caxton; and other historical events that influenced language change. For beginning readers, slowly developing their own phonic code of the more common spellings of sounds seems wiser than using already completed charts such as that developed for Words in Colour. To help sharpen detailed and accurate visual discrimination of words and awareness of language structure, young readers can list and group contractions to see how they are related to natural talk, find out what the apostrophe is replacing and, thus, stimulate more fluent reading. Older children can study effects of intonation—pauses, stress, and changes of pitch—research that should increase oral fluency and lead to an awareness of the limitations of writing.

In one fifth grade, where research ideas are being tried, the teacher asked each child to select two research areas out of nine grouped under three main categories: sounds, words, and syntax. Children were expected to pick their two areas on the basis of need for improvement. Each child chose a partner (who knew him well, but not as best friend) to examine the choices and write underneath "agree" or "disagree." Finally, the teacher (who knew all the children) studied all choices and conferred with a few children who did not seem aware of their own needs. Using the results, groups were formed to work on the various research topics. On the other hand, the whole class may be given a task, or volunteers requested for special ideas. For example, four girls volunteer-ed to try to find out what words are used most in the language. Students who could benefit from the writing practice of chart making were selected to make four charts showing the vowels, dipthongs, voiced consonants, and unvoiced consonants that the sound searching team had found. The only sound they missed was the vowel sound as heard in **put** and **foot.** Charts were made showing the symbols the various children had picked to stand for each sound. Then, using the glossaries in readers, spellers, language books, and workbooks, as well as the several dictionaries in the room, the students compared symbols used in these official sources with those chosen by the children.

Certainly, other means can be used to tie research ideas into the curriculum. Living in a world of knowledge, any curriculum is only an arbitrary sampling of the total available knowledge, so that many choices are available. School patterns and individual teaching styles will determine how research activities will be put to use, but any form of organization—team, self-contained, traditional, open, nongraded—can lend itself to research as a tactic for learning.

Comprehensiveness

As described above, children were asked to choose from three categories containing nine specific areas: 1) **Sounds**—hearing speech sounds accurately, pronouncing and articulating sounds in speech, and associating sounds and symbols in spelling and reading; 2) **Words**—recognizing, pronouncing, and understanding words; and 3) **Syntax**—writing or talking more, writing or talking clearly, and knowing when to use certain expressions. (It is not presumed all acitvity will be centered on research projects.) The foregoing areas were defined on the basis of some knowledge of linguistics, together with a survey of the texts being used. Thus, each child's particular needs can be included. For example, the children assigned to use of certain expressions will be studying usage, with the concept of one person's talk varying according to both his mood and the situation. Slang and dialect will be collected. Listening to interviews to note variations in the spontaneous responses of well-known individuals, or visits to local council meetings or court sessions will provide raw data for research.

Investigation quickly reveals language interrelationships. Structure leads into history, word formation, word origins, and spelling. Dialect relates to usage, vocabulary, sounds, and appropriateness, as well as differences between talk and written language. Oral fluency is increased by applying the notion of the structural grammarians that sentences are composed of a series of embedded immediate constituents. Sensing these pairings can lead to more meaningful phrasing, emphasis, and pauses; to concepts of noun and verb phrases (subject and predicate in traditional terminology); and to factors, other than vocabulary, that contribute to meaning. Through attention to kinesics—gesture and grimace—students recognize that much of language is unspoken.

Conclusion

Research by Children can overcome some of the linguistic and motivational weaknesses in reading and language programs. It is easy to discover that English derived from a Germanic tongue. Harder to understand is the concept that language is first of all speech, and that writing developed from speech. Letters don't have sounds, and a study of the nearly 400 spellings for the 40 American English speech sounds is one way to realize this fact. For example, there are at least twenty-eight ways to spell the unaccented vowel sound, **schwa.** Writing is not to be downgraded but, rather, to be put in correct perspective. If a screen, such as Latin Grammar or the misconception that writing either does or should determine speech, is erected between children and language, it is no wonder some children have difficulties in school. Research and investigation from primary sources is one way for children to penetrate that screen.

Sources for Students and Teachers

1. Brown, A. F. (Comp). **Normal and Reverse English Word List**, Air Force Office of Scientific Research, University of Pennsylvania, Philadelphia (9 volumes).
2. Burling, R. **English in Black and White**. New York: Holt, Rinehart and Winston, 1973.
3. DeLancey, R. W. **Linguistics and Teaching**, Monograph no. 9, New York State English Council.
4. Fries, C. **Linguistics and Reading**. New York: Holt, Rinehart and Winston.
5. Gattegno, C. Phonic Code, a part of his Words in Colour Reading System.
6. Hall, R. A., Jr. **Linguistics and Your Language**. New York: Doubleday Anchor.
7. Hanna, P., et al. **Phoneme-Grapheme Correspondences as Cues to Spelling Improvement**. HEW, USOE, US Government Printing Office, 1966 (OE 32008).
8. Jesperson, O. **Growth and Structure of the English Language**. New York: Doubleday Anchor.
9. Joos, M. **The Five Clocks**. New York: Harcourt Brace Jovanovich.
10. Laird, C. **The Miracle of Language**. New York: Fawcett Premier.
11. Mawson, C.O.S. **Dictionary of Foreign Terms.**New York: Bantam Books.
12. Nebraska Curriculum Development Center, **A Curriculum for English**, University of Nebraska Press, 1965.
13. Nist, J. **A Structural History of English**. New York: St. Martin's Press, 1966.
14. Ogg, O. **The 26 Letters**. New York: Thomas Y. Crowell.
15. **Oxford Universal Dictionary on Historical Principles**. New York: Oxford University Press.
16. Postman, N., Morine, and Morine. **Discovering Your Language**. New York: Holt, Rinehart and Winston, 1963.
17. Pyles, T. **The Origin and Development of the English Language**. Harcourt Brace Jovanovich, 1964.
18. Random House **Vest Pocket Rhyming Dictionary**.
19. Robertson, S., and Cassidy. **The Development of Modern English** (second edition). Englewood Cliffs, New Jersey: Prentice-Hall, 1954.
20. Rogers, J. R. (Ed.). **Linguistics in Reading Instruction**. University of Mississippi Reading Clinic.
21. **Say it In** _____ (French, Russian, Italian, Spanish, Japanese, German, Greek, Hebrew, Yiddish, etc.). New York: Dover Publications.
22. Strang, M.B.M. **Modern English Structure**. New York: St. Martin's Press, 1963.
23. **Thorndike, Barnhart Dictionary**, inside cover.
24. Webster, N. **A Compendious Dictionary of the English Language**, recently published in a facsimile of the first (1806) edition by Bounty Books, division of Crown Publishers.
25. **Webster's Seventh New Collegiate Dictionary**. "A Guide to Pronunciation," 16a-21a.
26. Wentworth, H., and S. Flexner. **Pocket Dictionary of American Slang**. New York: Pocket Books.

ADDITIONAL SOURCES: METHODS

Dale, E., et al. **Techniques of Teaching Vocabulary.** Reading, Massachusetts: Field Educational Publications (imprint of Addison-Wesley), 1971.
More appropriate for older students. Contains hundreds of activities for developing abilities in context clues, synonyms and antonyms, word origins, word roots, affixes, pronunciation and spelling, and figures of speech.

Dorsey, M.E. **Reading Games and Activities.** Belmont, California: Fearon Publishers, 1972.
At least 200 activities and games organized by skill areas. Emphasis on early elementary levels.

Hall, N. A. **Rescue.** Educational Service, Box 219, Stevensville, Michigan 49127, 1969.
About 200 ideas and activities for remedial reading teachers.

Heilman, A. W., and E. A. Holmes. **Smuggling Language Into the Teaching of Reading.** Columbus, Ohio: Charles E. Merrill, 1972.
About 100 activities, each with a stated purpose, organized according to skill areas. Based almost entirely on communicating and receiving messages; i.e., a meaning emphasis.

Herr, S. E. **Learning Activities for Reading** (second edition). Dubuque, Iowa: Wm. C. Brown, 1970.
Contains guide to grouping, plus 155 activities for grades one through six.

Koppman, P. **Language Arts Unlimited.** Greater San Diego Reading Association, San Diego, California, 1974.
About 100 language and reading activities for primary level.

Platts, M.E. **Spice.** Educational Service, Box 219, Stevensville, Michigan 49127, 1960.
About 200 language arts activities for grades one through six.

Platts, M. E. **Anchor.** Educational Service, Box 219, Stevensville, Michigan 49127, 1970.
About 200 vocabulary discovery activities for grades four through eight.

Russell, D., and E. Karp. **Reading Aids through the Grades** (revised). New York: Teachers College Press, 1975.
About 300 activities in reading for grades one through eight.

Spache, E. B. **Reading Activities for Child Involvement.** Boston: Allyn and Bacon, 1976.
Lists 472 reading activities for elementary grades. Well organized and very popular with teachers.

Note: This list includes only a few of the collections of activities available for use by teachers of language arts and reading. Although the activities can be very practical for busy teachers, they should not be used randomly merely because they are immediately available or fun to do. Rather, each activity should be carefully selected and prescribed for individuals or groups within the context of the diagnostic/prescriptive model as described in this volume.

MATERIALS

EVALUATION

INSTRUCTIONAL PURPOSE

METHODS

Management

In diagnostic/prescriptive instruction, individual growth within the group requires that different students do different things for varying lengths of time. The classroom teacher is faced with the task of organizing methods and materials, times and tasks, and places and people to create a learning environment that is orderly without being rigid, flexible without being chaotic.

What management skills are necessary in a center of such diverse activity? Students must be taught the basic classroom rules for using time, seeking assistance, and moving from place to place. They must be helped to discover their individual strengths and needs; be shown where to find materials and activities to use for various purposes; and be provided with optional activities to engage in when prescriptive tasks are finished, since finishing times will vary.

If aides are available, their time must be planned for maximum benefit. Attractive and functional centers of activity must be identified or created. Still another aspect of effective management is a systematic method for recording the needs, planned activities, and accomplishments of individuals and groups, with progress evaluation by each student as well as by the teacher.

In Section Five, the authors present ideas that are helpful in managing a classroom which fosters both independence and responsibility. One or more of these ideas may enhance your ability to deliver the often delicate balance of learning opportunities that individuals need if they are to move steadily and swiftly toward reading maturity.

Continuous Progress:
A Management System

MARTIN C. GOTOWALA
Connecticut Department of Education

In spite of all that has been written about the management of individualized reading programs and the numerous materials and instructional aids available commercially, teachers continue to experience difficulty in individualizing skills instruction. Probably the major reason for this difficulty is the lack of organization in the instructional process. In order to set up and maintain an individualized reading program, the classroom teacher must employ some type of management system that will enable him/her to diagnose the needs of each student, prescribe instruction based on the student's needs, and provide the necessary instruction through flexible grouping strategies.

A continuous progress organization provides the kind of well-structured reading program in which every student, regardless of age, will be at that point where he, as an individual, needs to be in an organized sequence of events in order to move forward with success. The student will be receiving the instruction he needs in the modality most suited to his learning style so that forward movement is continuous and at his built-in rate of absorption. This type of management system is not dependent upon any specific materials to hold the reading program together (e.g., basal programs). Rather, the unifying structure is to be found in a clear statement of instructional purpose.

Performance Objectives

There are five components of a continuous progress organization of a reading program. First, the specific skills to be taught must be stated as performance objectives. The role of performance objectives in a reading program is still a mystery to some teachers, although everyone is busy writing objectives and then trying to decide what to do with them.

They are the same objectives teachers have always written except they are stated in terms of what the student will be able to do as a result of instruction, instead of what the teacher will teach. For example:

Teacher Objective   To teach the short sound of the vowel ă.

Performance Objective   Given a list of ten unfamiliar one-syllable words containing examples of the short sound of the vowel ă, the student will read these words.

Performance objectives permit the establishment of a student-centered curriculum based on mastery because the objectives must be expressed in terms of the student's behavior at mastery, not the teacher's behavior during instruction. This feature also promotes diagnostic and flexible instructional procedures by giving the teacher greater freedom to teach without losing sight of the desired outcome.

Criterion Referenced Tests

Second, each performance objective must be accompanied by a criterion-referenced test (though not necessarily a paper and pencil test) to determine whether students have mastered the objective. Usually, this means several tests for any given objective because the same skill must be measured at several grade or age levels and provision must be made for retests. Criterion-referenced tests are different from standardized tests in that they provide an estimate of how much a student knows or has learned as measured against, a specified standard or criterion. A standardized (norm-referenced) test provides an estimate of how much a student knows or has learned through a comparison of his performance with the performance of others. Criterion-referenced tests are similar to the informal tests of specific skills which teachers have always written; the tests just have a new name. Criterion-referenced tests must be carefully written because a great deal depends on the use made of them.

Record Keeping

The third component of continuous progress is some kind of a record keeping system. This system must provide a way of keeping the results of the many criterion-referenced tests in a format which will serve as a continuing record of an individual child's progress as he masters one specific skill after another. Records tell the teacher which children need help with which skills, thereby serving as a charted course for carrying out the procedures in the classroom.

Materials

The fourth component is a key to the materials with which the skills can be taught. For example, if a child needs help with the short vowels, the teacher needs to know exactly where to go to find materials with which the child can work in order to learn these skills. Without this information in a well orgainized form, the teacher will waste valuable time. It is quite obvious that this approach leads to a use of materials very different from the procedures most teachers are used to. Instead of choosing a text or workbook and teaching it consecutively, the teacher will be assigning parts of these materials to individual children or groups and, perhaps, never using all of anything in any given text with any given student.

Management System

The last component essential to a continuous progress organization is a classroom management system. This component is by far the most difficult of the five to design and implement. The first four components can be developed either locally by a school district or purchased from a publisher. The classroom management system, however, is the area where teachers encounter the greatest difficulty in implementing a continuous progress program.

Assume that a school district has developed and/or purchased the first four components. The classroom teacher will have a set of performance objectives, accompanied by criterion-referenced tests. The children have taken the tests, the initial record or profile of each child has been drawn up, and the materials existing in the school have been keyed to the objectives. The teacher is now faced with approximately twenty-five individual student profiles showing the achievement (or lack of it) of all of the students on all the criterion-referenced tests they have taken. These data present a good diagnostic picture and provide a great deal of information about the needs of each student. But chances are that no two of these profiles will be exactly the same, and this is the point at which many teachers panic. There are very few teachers who have had any specific training in dealing with this complex problem in classroom organization.

Flexible Grouping

At this point, individual tutoring is impossible without budgetary increases which would be astronomical. Flexible grouping strategies should be employed to deal with the situation. The grouping strategies employed by each teacher do not have to be the same and, indeed, they probably couldn't be, given the varying potentialities and personalities of teachers.

The following general descriptions may suggest to teachers some ways in which they can begin to structure their own plans.

Strategy 1	Develop a series of **group contracts** related to the specific skills to be taught. Meet frequently with the groups to check progress, encourage sharing, and provide instruction in the skills involved in the contract. Each contract will specify the materials to be used and much of the work will be independent.
Strategy 2	Develop **individual contracts** related to any specific skills with which the student needs help. Check progress and give help on an individual basis. Care must be taken that the children carrying out these individual contracts also meet as groups; superficial learning results when children interact too little with each other and with the teacher.
Strategy 3	Set up **learning stations**—as many as there are skills to be emphasized at any one time. The learning stations require a lot of space in the classroom. Equip each station with materials needed, most of them self-instructional. Assign students to stations according to need. Allow them to choose which of the materials at the station they will use. Circulate among the stations, helping, evaluating, and determining when students may move to another station. Set up new stations when existing stations are no longer needed.
Strategy 4	Develop **team teaching** plans so that each teacher is responsible for certain skills in the hierarchy, Assign students temporarily to teachers responsible for certain needed skills. Reassign to other teachers as appropriate. This procedure limits the range of skills with which any one teacher must cope. However, it is harder to show students the application of the skills in the content areas when one has not been personally involved in teaching the skills to the students.
Strategy 5	Train **teacher aides**, volunteer or paid, to handle procedures for practicing specific skills. Stagger reading periods in the various rooms over the school day so that aides may work in more than one classroom. After the teacher has given the basic initial or review instruction in a given skill, aides can monitor the practice and the retesting. The keys to the effectiveness of this strategy are good practice materials and carefully trained aides.

Each of the above strategies presumes that the teacher has the profiles which identify the specific strengths and weaknesses of individual children in the classroom and that he/she has decided where to begin. As students' needs in relation to any given skill are met, the teacher discontinues working with the ad hoc group which has focused on this skill and reorganizes the children to meet some other need they have demonstrated. This process of organizing and reorganizing goes on continuously. Some children may need only one lesson to review or relearn a skill; others may need much more time.

Conclusion

Flexibility, of course, is the key concept. For some teachers used to traditional procedures, this is a difficult concept. Movement into any flexible skills management system must occur only after teachers have had plenty of time to think the plan through, collect or prepare materials, arrange classrooms for flexible grouping procedures, and adjust their thinking to what may prove to be quite a different climate in their classrooms. Supervisors and consultants, also, should move slowly into this type of program, for the teachers with whom they work will need strong support and, frequently, direct help with the operation of their classrooms.

A continuous progress program can be started at any grade level. Based on an analysis of the school district's need for change and the readiness of the teachers at any given level, a well-reasoned decision can be made as to the ideal entry point. Once begun, continuous progress can move up or down the sequence of skills or, perhaps, in both directions at once. It can be initiated on a voluntary basis with only those teachers who choose to participate or, after careful preparation, it can be implemented on a total-school or total-district basis. The program can be initiated with multiple materials or with a single basal (the basal being used quite differently—not page by page, but assigned and taught as individual student profiles indicate the need). Success does not depend so much on where or how the process begins, but on how carefully it is planned and monitored.

Management Systems and Open Classrooms

JONE P. WRIGHT
Auburn University

Reading is believed to be the most important academic skill that a child acquires in the elementary school. Hence, any legitimate elementary school places high priority upon reading success for the individual child. While there is consensus among educators that reading instruction should be improved, there seems to be almost no agreement about the direction in which improvement lies. The open classroom and management systems in reading are rapidly being adopted by elementary schools throughout the United States. After a perfunctory glance at these two innovations, one might conclude that they are diametrically opposite. The concept of a management system in reading may be a highly organized and structured skills program while the concept of an open school may suggest a program in which skills are not directly taught. However, the combination or coexistence of these two developments seems to hold great promise. For example, the complexity of the learning environment and flexible grouping in the open school mandate constant formative evaluation, a prime characteristic of management systems in reading.

Open Classroom

Reading in the open school movement is adeptly described by Sylvia Ashton-Warner in **Spinster** (1:40).

> ...What a dangerous activity reading is: teaching is. All this plastering of foreign stuff. Why plaster on at all when there's so much inside already? So much locked in? If only I could get it out and use it as working material. And not draw it out either. If I had a light enough to see, it would just come out under its own volcanic power.

The teacher not only encourages suggestions from children, but provides a rich and stimulating environment for learning. The demands on the resourcefulness and time of the teacher are colossal. Her task is to guide the children within parameters she has established. Since a pre-scribed procedure and text are not used, the teacher must constantly evaluate the worth and relevance of activities chosen by the children.

A common misconception is that there is no direct teaching of reading in the open school. Direct teaching of reading and phonics can be observed; however, discrete skills are taught in the context of the child's interest. There is a great deal of incidental teaching of phonics as the individual child develops word lists and writes stories or books. Phonics is not taught in isolation, but within the context of what the children are reading and writing. There may be some formal teaching from a basal series, but the children are allowed to select much of their reading materials. However, the direct teaching from a basal is only one small part of the reading activities carried on in the open school.

The children assume responsibility for selecting books and activities within the rich environment the teacher has established. The children are free to move about the room. They may discuss with friends the books they are reading or may evaluate the books they are reading. They are not forced to answer ten questions about each book read. The teacher does not hear the children read from a single text in a predetermined circle. Grouping is flexible and the children choose a story which they read and discuss together. Books are evident everywhere: trade books, textbooks, and books made by the children. A publishing center, where young authors bind and illustrate books they have written, is often found in the open school. The children may report to the teacher by making a tape or mural, or engaging in creative dramatics. In summary, a characteristic of the open school is that children accept responsibility to carry on by themselves rather than to sit passively while the teacher gives directions.

Another common misconception concerning reading in the open school is that the reading is boisterous and wild. There is always "work noise" rather than dead quiet. The children engage in activities they want to complete because they choose the activities. For example, five children may be busy reading directions to make a pinhole camera; they are intrigued that they may be able to construct a camera that will work. The work noise they make is understandable. The children give and receive advice from their peers, as well as from the teacher. They read and reread the directions. They achieve mastery of almost every word in the directions because they want to make a camera that really works.

Some children are designing paper airplanes and helicopters from printed directions; other children are writing directions so they may share an original design. Others are constructing covers and bindings for their latest books, while another group discusses a newspaper report of the latest UFO landing. Several children are lying on a rug reading trade books they have selected and other children are working with an abacus, while others are near the science center describing the movements of ant colonies in the ant farm. One child is writing the teacher a letter suggesting activities for the next week.

Children move about the room when the teacher is present as well as when she is absent. Children are allowed to secure and replace materials. Books, writing paper, and other necessary items are stored so the children who use them need no assistance in reaching or returning materials. The children are growing in self-reliance and self-discipline. The atmosphere is happy and relaxed, but also purposeful and business-like.

Management Systems

Management systems are assuming increasing importance in reading instruction. The commercially prepared packages range from complex to relatively simple designs. Almost every system now on the market contains four common elements: a series of behaviorally stated performance objectives or specific reading skills, instruments for assessing skill mastery and skill needs, a compendium of teaching resources, and a series of instruments that will serve as posttests.

The diagnostic devices are criterion-referenced rather than standardized instruments. Mastery of the skill as expressed in the behavioral objective is the important criterion. These instruments permit a relatively inexperienced teacher to assess a child's skill needs. In fact, some of the answer sheets are devised to offer a diagnostic profile on the answer sheet when a carbon paper is removed. Grading the child's test and the development of a tentative profile are accomplished in a few seconds. After studying and modifying the suggested profile, the teacher may plan instruction based on skill weaknesses or strengths of individual children.

If the teacher has no specific resource in mind, she may locate a list of materials or suggestions in the compendium or resource guide. After planning and guiding appropriate activities, the teacher administers the posttest to the child or children involved. Groups of children must be quite flexible so that children who master the skill are regrouped in a manner that reflects their further skill needs.

A faculty serious about the use of a management system inventories all of the resources for reading instruction. The resources are consolidated in a central location in the elementary school building, where they are accessible to all teachers and children. After this process is complete, the faculty can then purchase new materials and media on a needs basis.

The systems approach in reading can be misused. In a recent observation, a teacher in a fourth year classroom administered a criterion-referenced test for the purpose of measuring auditory discrimination of labial sounds in the final position. Before the results were collected, the teacher passed out five duplicated worksheets related to this skill. The teacher had not used the test results to gain further knowledge of the children's mastery of the skill. Rather, the worksheets were "prescribed" for each child with no regard to individual needs or wishes. If the child had mastered the skill, he was handed five sheets of review, practice, or busy work. No instructional strategy was suggested for the child who needed instruction. Yet the teacher expressed concern that the children were not interested in reading and were not improving!

Thus, some children may be drilled on skills which they have already mastered. Others may be frustrated—constantly urged to try harder without guidance of identified skill deficiencies and the necessary prescriptions. Proper use of management systems can alleviate these conditions.

A misconception concerning the systems approach is that of a harsh classroom climate. To some people, the very term **systems** implies a cold, mechanical approach to the teaching of reading. A systems approach can allow the humane teacher to develop a rather complete profile of student weaknesses and strengths and to individualize instruction by providing appropriate materials and activities.

Conclusion

Management systems in reading will no doubt continue to be adopted by many schools. If the approach is to be successful, reading instruction and personnel must change in several ways. The classroom teacher must 1) possess adequate knowledge of reading skills and the novel ways to present them, 2) provide many alternative activities from which children may learn, and 3) arrange an appealing learning environment so that children are encouraged to read. Also, the classroom teacher, the reading specialist, and the administrator must permit children to progress vertically into objectives and curriculum materials commonly prescribed for higher grades.

Can two innovative developments—management systems and open classrooms—coexist? A rich and stimulating learning environment for children, adequate knowledge of reading on the part of the teacher, and flexible grouping of children are characteristics of both. The systems approach in reading vitally needs the natural informality of the open school. The open school movement will surely profit from the systematic skills approach of management systems in reading.

Reference

1. Ashton-Warner, Sylvia. **Spinster**. New York: Simon and Schuster, 1958.

Learning Stations and the Reading Class

EILEEN VARDIAN DUVAL
Ballast Point Elementary School
Tampa, Florida

ROGER E. JOHNSON
University of South Florida

JOHN LITCHER
Wake Forest University

This discussion suggests teacher assistance in four basic areas involving setting up and using learning stations in the classroom:

1. Use of Classroom Space
2. Planning Classroom Time
3. Record Keeping
4. Evaluation of Achievement

Although the construction of learning stations is not discussed, two simple stations—**Freddy Frog** and **Reading Stories for Comprehension**—are provided at the end of the paper to serve as examples.

Use of Classroom Space

When considering learning stations in a room the teacher must remember that each classroom is unique. One merely needs to assess what materials are available for use and then let imagination take over. **What** is placed in the room and **how** it is placed help to determine the atmosphere for learning. Every part of the room is important. It must allow freedom of movement as well as freedom to experiment and/or discover.

The teacher must utilize room space so as to create areas which provide a balance between: quiet and noisy work; independent study and group interaction; and materials storage and the display of individual and group accomplishments. Sectioning parts of the room into working areas and stations helps to make more efficient use of classroom space and also creates an environment which encourages learning. When assessing what is available within a classroom, a teacher may wish to consider some of the following suggestions for utilizing space.

1. A temporary **room divider** can be made by hanging cloth, with pieces of toweling glued to each end, from the ceiling of the classroom. (This is only to set aside a part of the room; it is not to make it into a completely private area.)
2. **Large cardboard boxes** can become portable offices, cubicles, or booths simply by cutting out parts of boxes.
3. **Closet doors,** if left open, can become bulletin boards, or screens for viewing films or filmstrips. Materials that children will be using can be stored inside the closet.
4. **Corrugated paper** can be used to design areas where students work independently, by taping it along a table top to form individual study booths.
5. An old **lampshade** is a good place to display activity sheets, directions for activities, and lists of activities or projects.
6. **Bottle boxes** with divided sections can be used to store labeled items such as maps, pictures, or dittoes.
7. An old **shoe holder** is good for storing supplies such as staplers, staples, rubber bands, pins, markers, pencils, and paper clips for easy accessibility.
8. **Boxes** of all sizes can be used for display areas, private reading booths, movie screens, and backdrops.
9. **Colored yarn,** stretched across the room, can become a handy line for displaying the work of students or groups.

A floor plan of the classroom made on a piece of oaktag, with each learning station designated, gives students the opportunity to see what is available for them to do. This also permits them to select what they want. Each student has a name flag which is placed at the learning station where work is being done. When finished, a student can see what stations are open and then move on.

Planning Classroom Time

Once a classroom is arranged in an acceptable manner, the next concern is that of planning classroom time. Teachers must keep in mind that the purpose of learning centers is to help students become independent and responsible learners and to increase awareness of their own abilities and interests. The planning device used should provide students with formats that assist them in budgeting their time, programming their learning, and making decisions from the choice of activities available to them. The type of schedule used will depend on the objectives or goals and the needs and capabilities of the students.

Each student's time can be planned in many ways, depending on individual and small group needs. A form of **rotational scheduling** (Figure 1) might be used to rotate groups of children to the stations. The outer circle in Figure 1 indicates the stations the teacher feels are important for the students. The inner circle, with names of students for each station, can be rotated daily, or after a work period of any appropriate length. Here, the teacher decides when students will go to the learning stations. What they will do when they get there may be prescribed by the teacher for some individuals and optional for others.

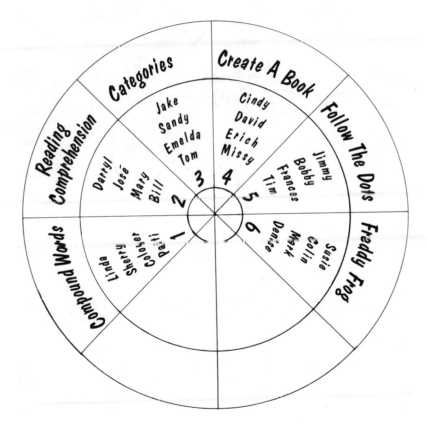

Figure 1.   Rotational Scheduling

One variation of rotational scheduling, of course, is to let each student decide when to go to the assigned station, as well as what to do there.

Trail scheduling (Figure 2) can be used to ensure that each student will experience station activities in a sequence assigned by the teacher.

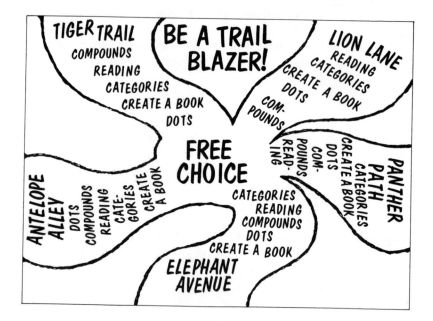

Figure 2.   Trail Scheduling

Many teachers use a form of **contracting** (Figure 3). This allows the student to state his choice of stations, when he will go there, and what he will do when he gets there.

Learning contracts permit students to contract with the teacher in order to get involved in a particular task. It is essential that, with such a contract, the student knows how much time he is allotted to work and what will happen if he does not fulfill his contract. A postcard can be developed with one side for use by the teacher to remind a student of activities to be completed, and the other side for the student to relate what has been done. A weekly schedule with some open time blocks can be designed, as well. Students fill in the open time blocks and turn the schedule in to the teacher. If the teacher approves, the students must fulfill their schedules much the same as with contracting.

The teacher's time plan depends on the type of student schedule

```
┌─────────────────────────────────────┐
│                                     │
│  Date_____        │
│                                     │
│  I agree to do the                  │
│  following things by                │
│  Date_____        │
│                                     │
│  _____        │
│                                     │
│  _____        │
│                                     │
│  _____        │
│                                     │
│  _____        │
│                                     │
│  _____        │
│                                     │
│       _____           │
│           Student's Name            │
│                                     │
│     ___Ms. E. Thurdian___           │
│                                     │
└─────────────────────────────────────┘
```

Figure 3.   Contracting

employed. Always, when teachers schedule their time they must consider the following as their priorities. What skills or subjects need to be taught? Who needs help? What can I do to motivate interest in a particular station? If time is allowed for teaching as well as for interaction and/or intervention with students, teacher planning time should be no problem.

Record Keeping

When using learning stations in the classroom, record keeping becomes very important. It provides the teacher with an account of what the students have been doing and in what things they need further help. It gives the students a sense of accomplishment as learners, and helps develop student responsibility to follow through on a given task. Record keeping also serves to provide parents with a comprehensive picture of what their child has been doing in the classroom. Figure 4 shows two simple record forms.

_____
DATE
Today I Did The Following:

_____
_____
_____
_____

_____
STUDENT'S NAME

WHAT HAVE YOU READ?

Date Started	Title of Book	Author	Date Finished	Comments

Figure 4.   Record Forms

Evaluation

Record keeping and evaluation are continuous and closely related. The former tells what has been accomplished and the latter tells how well it has been accomplished. In the learning station approach to teaching, the goal of evauation is to increase student responsibility for self-evaluation. It is the teacher's responsibility to plan the method and the time for evaluation as well as to teach the student how to evaluate. Academic growth as well as personal growth should be evaluated and can be done either orally or in writing, depending on the student and the activity. Figure 5 shows examples of simple (but effective) forms for student self-evaluation.

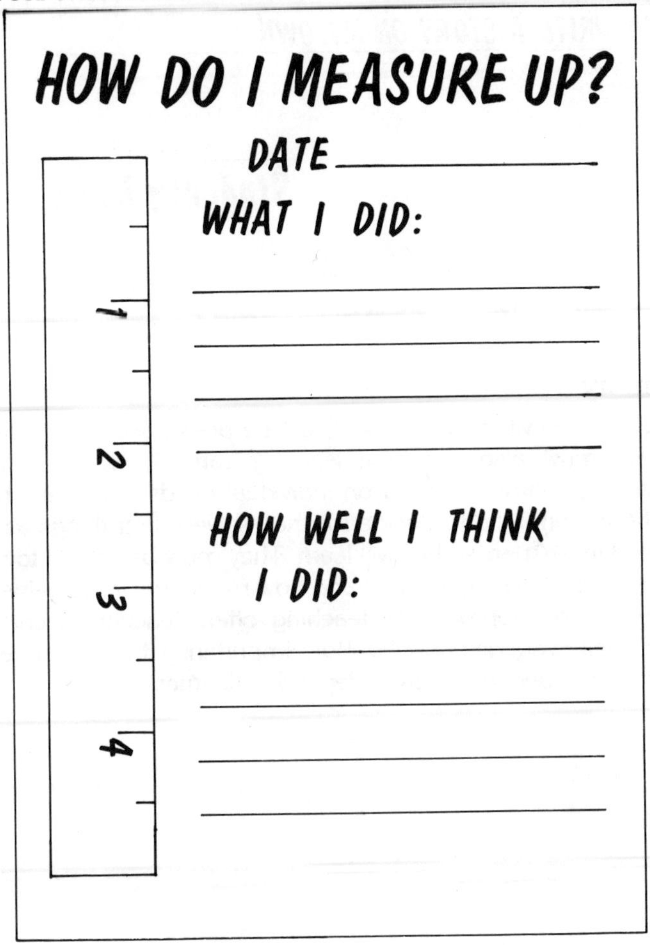

HOW DO I MEASURE UP?

DATE _____

WHAT I DID:

_____
_____
_____
_____

HOW WELL I THINK
I DID:

_____
_____
_____
_____

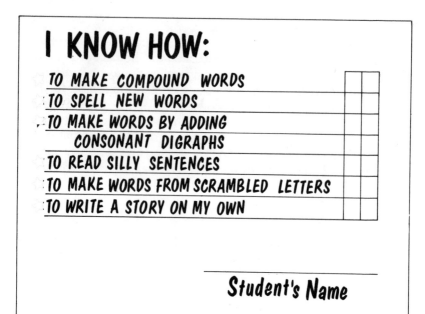

I KNOW HOW:

TO MAKE COMPOUND WORDS		
TO SPELL NEW WORDS		
TO MAKE WORDS BY ADDING CONSONANT DIGRAPHS		
TO READ SILLY SENTENCES		
TO MAKE WORDS FROM SCRAMBLED LETTERS		
TO WRITE A STORY ON MY OWN		

Student's Name

Figure 5. Self-Evaluation Forms

Summary

Some activities, of course, must be prescribed for all students. Teachers must also supervise learning carefully, and continue to evaluate that learning. Based on individual needs, however, students must be encouraged to decide for themselves such things as when, what, and in what order they will learn. They must be helped to ponder how well they have participated and how much they have gained. The learning station approach to teaching offers teachers a chance to expand their professional skills. More importantly it offers students an opportunity to become more independent learners.

PLAN FOR A LEARNING CENTER

Name of Center: **FREDDY FROG**   Date: September 1973

OBJECTIVE   To provide students with practice in forming words by filling
   in the blanks with a consonant digraph.

PROCEDURE

   What You Need: Paper and Pencil.

   What You Do: 1. Pick a card.
                           2. Read the directions on the card.
                           3. Write your answers on your own
                              paper; DO NOT write on the card.
                           4. Return the card to the folder.
                           5. Turn in your work.

MATERIALS   Precut frog shaped cards with consonant digraph and words
   written on them and then laminated. Paper and pencil.

EVALUATION Children enjoy being able to pick the card they would like to
   work with. Activities provide opportunities to draw pictures, write
   sentences, or tape stories.

PLAN FOR A LEARNING CENTER

READING STORIES FOR
Name of Center: **COMPREHENSION**   Date: September 1973

OBJECTIVE   To provide students with opportunities to pick stories they
would like to read and then to do follow-up activities based on what
they read.

PROCEDURE

What You Need: A wax crayon.

What You Do: 1. Pick a folder that you would like to
                        work in.
                        2. Read the book.
                        3. Answer the questions on the pages
                        inside the folder.
                        4. See your teacher when you are finished.

MATERIALS   Paperback books, questions and vocabulary work in a folder,
wax crayon.

EVALUATION Good activity for encouraging independent reading.

Duval, Johnson, and Litcher

Becza, J. "Reading Management Systems: An Instructional Sequence Concern," **Reading Instruction Journal**, June 1976. Westfield, New Jersey: New Jersey Reading Teachers Association, 62, 70-71.

> Here is a clear description of diagnostic/prescriptive instruction ("test, teach, practice, test") and a clearly worded caution at the ease with which the teaching step can be omitted and replaced with more testing.

Blomberg, I. E. "Tip Your Teaching of Reading toward the Learning Center Approach," **Indiana Reading Quarterly**, Fall 1972, 8-14.

> The author explains the concept of learning centers, shows how to begin and plan learning center activities, suggests ideas for reading learning centers, and lists a number of helpful annotated references.

Gold, P., and A. M. Taylor. "Of Course, Volunteers," **Reading Teacher**, April 1975, 614-616.

> This is a good brief outline for training and using volunteers in a reading program for instruction (providing practice, assisting individuals, reading to kids) and for evaluation (monitoring testing, helping score tests, recording results). Several helpful references are listed, as well.

Johnson, D. D., and P. D. Pearson. "Skills Management Systems: A Critique," **Reading Teacher**, May 1975, 757-764.

> Here are "six things that bother us about skills management systems." A careful consideration of these six things is essential for every teacher in organizing for diagnostic/prescriptive instruction.

Olds, A. R. "Making Hard Rooms Soft Rooms," **Learning**, November 1972, 36-40.

> The author explains how to change a bare, unappealing, "hard"classroom into an attractive and functional learning environment with a minimum of artistic and carpentry skills and lots of free or inexpensive materials. The easily possible changes in color, texture, and space are exciting to behold, as the many photographs prove.

Stauffer, R. G., and M. M. Harrell. "Individualizing Reading-Thinking Activities," **Reading Teacher**, May 1975, 765-769.

> The authors present detailed instructions for organizing individual and small group research designed to answer children's own questions on topics of interest.

Vacca, R. T., and J. L. Vacca. "Consider a Stations Approach to Middle School Reading Instruction," **Reading Teacher**, October 1974, 18-21.

> The Vaccas describe a learning station approach that combines prescriptive tasks with self-selection by the students. They list four guidelines useful in governing student activity and movement. Several of their twelve learning stations are described briefly. Most importantly, the scheduling is described in detail.

Perspective Two

The development of reading maturity is, in many ways, a very personal process. So it is also with the development of the ability to teach reading. This volume has presented only a small sample of ideas designed to help teachers increase their competence in diagnostic/prescriptive classroom practice. These ideas, the additional sources listed throughout, and any other available information, must be explored, evaluated, and assimilated if each reader is to develop his/her full professional potential.

In addition to ideas of a practical nature, some organizing framework or cognitive structure must be employed to make sense of a mass of specific techniques, in order to identify and clarify the larger and more important concept—an effective instructional sequence. In this volume, that organizing framework has been supplied in the form of a diagnostic/prescriptive model of reading instruction. In developing and perfecting your teaching ability, the diagnostic/prescriptive model is one organizational structure; it is important to explore other means of instructional implementation, as well.

Given a serious and purposeful examination of the almost infinite number of specific teaching ideas, as well as the several instructional models, the reader of this volume will emerge as a more knowledgeable and more effective teacher of reading. The present volume does not attempt to provide that knowledge, but merely to enlarge it; not to create that effectiveness, but merely to enhance it.

One final note: Concern with the instructional program in reading can easily overshadow or even eclipse the fun and informational reading so necessary if students are to become fluent and mature readers. Direct instruction, therefore, is but **one** element of a complete reading program. At least equal emphasis in the best classrooms is placed on the actual use of reading—for fun and information—in real situations for real purposes. These two additional emphases—recreational and functional reading—are given only passing mention in the present volume.

RAE

Earle

FUNCTIONAL READING

INSTRUCTIONAL READING

RECREATIONAL READING

121

The International Reading Association attempts, through its publications, to provide a forum for a wide spectrum of opinion on reading. This policy permits divergent viewpoints without assuming the endorsement of the Association.